The Public Policy Pri

This short guide provides a concise and accessible overview of the entire policy cycle, taking the reader through the various stages of agenda setting, policy formulation, decision-making, policy implementation, and policy evaluation.

Public officials at every level of government play a vital role in the development, adoption, and implementation of government policies. Yet most existing works focus only on the most senior politicians and public officials and, thus, often fail to provide an insight into the work of the vast majority of other officials. This book provides an introduction to key policy functions, the challenges they entail, and how these challenges may be addressed by mid-level and other public officials. Written from a comparative perspective, the authors include examples from a diverse range of countries at different stages of development, highlighting key principles and practices through which officials can effectively manage their policy processes and outcomes.

This important tool offers both students and practitioners of public policy guidance on how to make, implement, and evaluate public policies in ways that improve citizens' lives.

Xun Wu is Associate Professor at the Lee Kuan Yew School of Public Policy at the National University of Singapore, specializing in policy reforms in developing countries, with emphasis on social and environmental sectors.

M. Ramesh is Professor of Social Policy at the University of Hong Kong. His teaching and research are concentrated in public policy, social policy, and political economy in Asia.

Michael Howlett is Burnaby Mountain Professor in the Department of Political Science at the Simon Fraser University, Canada and teaches in the Lee Kuan Yew School of Public Policy at the National University of Singapore. His areas of specialization include public policy analysis, political economy, and resource and environmental policy.

Scott A. Fritzen is Associate Professor and Vice-Dean of the Lee Kuan Yew School of Public Policy, National University of Singapore, and specializes in governance reform and capacity strengthening in developing countries.

Routledge Textbooks in Policy Studies

This series provides high-quality textbooks and teaching materials for upper-level courses on all aspects of public policy as well as policy analysis, design, practice, and evaluation. Each text is authored or edited by a leading scholar in the field and aims both to survey established areas and present the latest thinking on emerging topics.

The Public Policy Primer
Managing the policy process
Xun Wu, M. Ramesh, Michael Howlett and Scott Fritzen

The Public Policy Primer

Managing the policy process

Xun Wu, M. Ramesh, Michael Howlett and Scott Fritzen

Routledge
Taylor & Francis Group

LONDON AND NEW YORK

First published 2010
by Routledge
2 Park Square, Milton Park, Abingdon, Oxon, OX14 4RN

Simultaneously published in the USA and Canada
by Routledge
711 Third Avenue, New York, NY 10017

*Routledge is an imprint of the Taylor & Francis Group,
an informa business*

© 2010 Xun Wu, M. Ramesh, Michael Howlett and Scott Fritzen

Typeset in Times New Roman by
Florence Production Ltd, Stoodleigh, Devon

British Library Cataloguing in Publication Data
A catalogue record for this book is available from the British Library

Library of Congress Cataloging in Publication Data
Wu, Xun.
  The public policy primer: managing the policy process/
  Xun Wu, M. Ramesh, Michael Howlett & Scott Fritzen.
     p. cm.—(Routledge textbooks in policy studies)
    1. Public policy.   2. Political planning.   3. Policy sciences.
  I. Howlett, Michael, 1955– II. Fritzen, Scott, 1969– III.
  Title.
  H97.W9 2010
  320.6—dc22   2010006072

ISBN13: 978–0–415–78046–9 (hbk)
ISBN13: 978–0–415–78047–6 (pbk)
ISBN13: 978–0–203–84594–3 (ebk)

Contents

Illustrations

Figures

Tables

Boxes

Acknowledgments

We are grateful to Fulai Sheng of the United Nations Environment Agency for giving us the opportunity to prepare a manual on policy-making for sustainable development. That project inspired us to write this textbook for a broader audience.

We are also grateful to many at the Lee Kuan Yew School of Public Policy at the National University of Singapore for their support for the project, especially Kishore Mahbubani, Hui Weng Tat, and Stavros Yiannouka. We have used portions of the manuscript in masters courses and executive education sessions at the School, and the response we received from students and trainees helped us tremendously: sincere thanks to all of you.

1 Public managers and the policy process

This book is for public managers concerned about their role in a policy world in which their efforts are often undermined or underappreciated by both their political executives and the general public. While the term "public managers" includes the elite echelons of government, consisting of ministers and heads of agencies, the intended main audience for the book is the vast and diverse group of career public servants who assume managerial positions at various levels in public sector organizations and who play an important role in designing and implementing public policies. These public managers often shoulder a disproportionately larger share of the public scrutiny for failures in public sector governance than they should, and our book is intended to assist them. It is built upon the premise that, informed by a better understanding of policy processes, public managers can overcome many of the barriers that undermine their potential for contributing to the policy process and, eventually, to policy success.

A fragmented policy world

Public policy occupies the center stage in the world of public managers, potentially providing them with both the legitimacy and resources they require in order to perform their tasks at a high level of intelligence, sophistication and competence. However, the policy process is often rife with irrationality, inconsistencies, and lack of coordination, all of which can become major sources of tension and distress for these officials. In particular, if public managers are unfamiliar with the nature and workings of the policy process, they may be unable to devise effective strategies for influencing its direction and ensuring it results in an integrated set of policy outcomes.

The following illustrations show that one need not travel far to encounter examples of policy problems caused by the existence of a fragmented policy world:

- *Ineffective but popular policies command the attention of policy-makers while many unpopular but necessary policies encounter severe resistance.* During the recent financial crisis, for example, many developing countries, for political reasons, had to continue providing subsidies that they could ill afford and that were counterproductive in terms of improving overall living conditions and standards.
- *Policy-making is driven by crises in which policy-makers must act as firefighters while policies to prevent the crises in the first place are undervalued.* In the UK and the US, for example, many of the banking practices that led to the 2008 financial crisis had their origin in the earlier deregulation of the financial industry whose short-comings were well known but ignored in the pursuit of economic growth.
- *Policy failures lead to changes in political leadership but the root causes of the failures remain inadequately addressed.* In many developing countries, leaders have rotated through periods of military and civilian governments without being able to address the basic problems—such as lack of skills and infrastructure—that hamper their development efforts.
- *The effects of policies championed by a particular government agency can be undermined by strategies employed by another agency, deliberately or otherwise.* Thus, for example, in countries such as India and Pakistan, agriculture ministries continue to promote agricultural production at the expense of decreased water availability for industry and households, which are themselves the subjects of major expenditure initiatives by ministries of public works and infrastructure.
- *Policies are formulated in order to secure the support of politically powerful groups at the expense of long-term public interests that are underrepresented in the political system.* In the Philippines, Mexico and many other countries, small groups of agricultural and business elites exercise a virtual veto over reforms aimed at redistributing land or improving wages and working conditions for the large majority of the population.
- *Disagreements between different levels of government lead to contradictory policies that are mutually destructive.* The goal of a future policy can be thoroughly clouded by different government agencies, at different levels of government, pursuing incompatible or contradictory agendas. In Canada and Australia, for example, federal and provincial or state-level governments can pursue mutually exclusive goals—for example, where one level promotes coal or oil and gas extraction to produce electric power while another level tries to reduce greenhouse gas emissions.

- *Policies implemented by street-level bureaucrats deviate considerably from what was envisaged at the policy formulation stage.* Local officials in many developing countries often override or subvert policies, not least by demanding and accepting payments for overlooking or amending rules. Even where corruption is less of a problem now than in the past, such as Indonesia, Taiwan, or Sri Lanka, such actions can easily lead to a confusing patchwork of rules and regulations, undermining the efficiency and effectiveness of many policies. Conversely, national policies (which may, for instance, be adopted for purposes of political signalling) may at times be so poorly conceived that they are practically "built to fail," regardless of implementation effort.

- *Despite its importance, policy evaluation is rarely used for most policy decisions, and, when it is conducted, it is motivated by procedural requirements or narrow political considerations and thus fails to contribute to continuous policy learning.* Numerous governments around the world regularly block access to information, depriving evaluators of the ability to conduct high quality evaluations and themselves of opportunities for policy learning and improvement.

The commonality of such fragmented policy processes across different political systems and regimes begs not only for explanation, but also for solutions that public managers can adopt when faced with these and other similar situations. These are what this book aims to provide.

Public managers as the missing link

Due to their prominent role in developing policy choices and implementing executive decisions, public managers as a whole tend to shoulder a large share of public scrutiny, and blame, for failures resulting from fragmented policy processes. They are often lumped together with the agencies they serve as "the bureaucracy," which in itself is seen in many circles as largely responsible for most failures in public sector governance. Because of their purported "bureaucratic incompetence" and "resistance to change," public managers are often blamed for poor policy formulation and weak implementation of policy initiatives. Their motivations and commitments are also frequently questioned. Much of the economics-inspired literature on bureaucratic behavior, for example, is based on the assumption that a typical public manager is largely motivated by his or her personal interests and/or narrowly defined institutional interests such as information or budget maximization in dealing with public affairs. The hostile political environment in which they operate in many countries further undermines the efforts of public managers and over time can give rise to popular demands for downsizing the government and transferring many public responsibilities to the private or non-profit sectors, further promoting policy fragmentation. The above views, however, contrast sharply with how the public managers themselves view their roles. Public managers tend to perceive their role as delivering high quality services or maintaining the government machinery (for example, policing the streets and collecting taxes) rather than contributing to policy-making. Many public managers, when they do think about the subject of policy-making at all, see their policy role as one limited to policy implementation, since they often feel, or have been trained to think, that policy-making is the sole responsibility of political decision-makers.

This narrow self-perception of the policy role of public managers is rooted in traditional public administration theories developed on the basis of Western experiences which historically have advocated a strong separation between administration and politics, with the latter belonging exclusively to the realm of political executives. Although the empirical and conceptual validity of the separation between administration and politics have been challenged by generations of scholars, its staying power in influencing administrative practices can be seen clearly from many key reform measures introduced as part of the New Public Management (NPM) adopted in many countries in the 1980s and 1990s. The NPM was an approach that often aimed to separate more clearly "policy-making" agencies from "implementation" agencies in order to boost administrative efficiency and effectiveness. In the Netherlands, for example, reforms in the 1990s created completely separate agencies for policy and administration.

In addition to the influence of traditional public administration theories, the perceived narrow policy role of public managers also arises from a misperception that equates "policy process" with "decision-making" (which often does involve, mainly or exclusively, more senior political executives). But the policy process consists of a much broader range of activities than merely making decisions. It includes setting agendas, developing alternatives, implementing decisions, and evaluating public measures—all tasks in which public managers can play a major part. And public managers can also play a bigger role in decision-making than is often realized. For example, policies adopted by legislators can be broad and vague (often deliberately so for political reasons), leaving crucial details to be decided by public managers, or street-level bureaucrats, when implementing them.

Several recent developments, moreover, have led to a renewed questioning of this historical "politics–administration dichotomy" and have reinforced the need to expand the definition of the appropriate policy roles that can be played by public managers.

First, decentralization and devolution have transferred critical policy roles to public managers at lower levels of governments in many countries. In countries ranging from the Philippines to Peru and Chile, for example, the responsibilities for major health policies have been devolved from the central government to local governments in recent years. Similarly, in the US and the EU, efforts to control global warming have increasingly shifted to regional and urban governments.

Second, the emergence of network or collaborative government practices built on participatory and consultative processes in many countries, especially in Europe and Latin America, has enlarged the scope of influence for public managers. Governance authority is no longer solely top-down, but often incorporates (often parallel) bottom-up processes in which they play a larger, more continuing role.

Third, the customer-orientation in public sector governance adopted in many jurisdictions under NPM rubrics, which has affected virtually every country from Argentina to Korea and Senegal, has also strengthened the voice and leverage of agencies that deliver goods and services to the public. In so doing, it may have strengthened the hand of the public managers who oversee such service delivery.

Through their expanded policy roles, public managers now more than ever can bring a set of qualities to policy deliberations and activities that can help contribute to solving many policy problems associated with fragmented policy practices. The long tenure of public managers in the public sector, for example, helps them not only sustain attention to particular policy issues, but also enables them to take a long-term perspective on public policy, which political executives facing electoral and other shorter-term pressures often lack. In comparison, policy-makers at the top level, such as ministers, legislators and governors, face much shorter tenures in office and find it correspondingly more difficult to influence the direction and content of policy-making over the long term. The job security and expertise enjoyed by public managers, especially career civil servants, also shields them from the political pressures (such as the need to win elections) that constrain political masters when dealing with policy issues. As a result, policy managers are able to both take a longer-term perspective on policy-making and give greater weight to technical considerations when devising and implementing policies. Additionally, the involvement of public managers is more likely to spread across multiple stages in the policy process, whereas the engagement of policy-makers at the top may be concentrated on certain specific stages (for example, agenda setting, decision-making, or evaluation), again providing public managers with more opportunities than politicians to affect policy content.

Public managers in the policy process: a framework for action

It would, however, be overly optimistic to think that simply expanding the policy roles of public managers will lead automatically to improvements in public sector governance. In Indonesia, for example, some analysts have found that decentralization of essential social services such as health and education has led in some lower-capacity localities to a noticeable deterioration in service quality, due to a lack of budgets and administrative skills, that has especially hurt the poor. Such an expanded policy role can prove overwhelming for ill-prepared public managers who lack either the experience and/or training in public policy-making to be able to anticipate both the threats and opportunities such circumstances might bring.

Proper training is essential for unleashing public managers' tremendous potential in tackling public problems. Unfortunately, the existing literatures in both public administration and the policy sciences provide little guidance on how to cultivate public managers' policy roles. Scholarly works on the policy process, for example, invariably take the perspective of outsiders observing the process rather than that of someone working within the system. The stages model of the policy process (from agenda setting to evaluation), for example, does not resonate with low- and mid-level public officials immersed in a messy and fragmented policy world in which they often see the stages overlapping and issues and problems intertwined. Only a few works in public administration attempt to provide any guidance at all for public managers on how to be more effective in their policy role, and even these are usually restricted to describing specific tools to use and strategies to adopt in specific circumstances related to leadership or human resource issues. And, while there are richer materials in political science, policy analysis, and public management about the nature of the political, technical, and organizational components of political and policy processes, there is no attempt to combine these literatures with a view to providing useful guidance to public managers on how they can integrate or balance these considerations in practice.

This book aims to address these shortcomings by providing public managers an action-oriented framework to guide their participation in the policy process (see Figure 1.1). The framework consists of three layers—policy functions, policy perspectives, and policy competencies

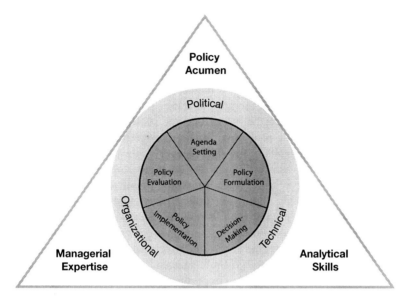

Figure 1.1 Influencing the policy process: an action-oriented framework for
public managers

—which public managers must understand in order to exercise their
capacity to influence, create, and pursue integrated policies in their
spheres of activity.

Policy functions

The general policy-making functions that public managers can undertake
consist of five essential activities: agenda-setting, formulation, decision-
making, implementation, and evaluation. In this conception, the policy
activities do not occur in "stages" with a linear progression from one
to the next. Rather, they are discrete, albeit interrelated, sets of activities that public managers can engage in to achieve their society's and
government's policy goals. A typical public manager may be heavily
involved in some policy-making activities, somewhat more involved in
others, and not at all in the rest. Policy managers can make a crucial
contribution to all of these policy functions, however, by leveraging on
their policy acumen, analytical skills, and managerial expertise.

1. *Agenda-setting.* Each society has literally hundreds of issues that
    some citizens find to be matters of concern and would have the

government do something about, of which only a small proportion is actually taken up in policy development. The role of public managers has often been underestimated in this area, as the spotlight has been focussed on policy-makers in executive and legislative branches of government, the media, and the general public. Public managers, however, are in a unique position to identify emerging policy issues through the programs they direct and the people they serve, often before the issues become problematic enough to be considered public problems. Public managers can also serve as a screening mechanism and "gatekeeper" able to substantiate and verify (or not) various claims for attention among policy-makers and the public at large. Most important, public managers can contribute to solving significant policy issues that require sustained attention through their long tenures in office.

2. *Policy formulation.* Policy formulation involves the development of alternatives for possible courses of government activity designed to address problems on the government agenda. Policy-makers typically face short-lived windows of opportunity to come up with actionable solutions due to competition for their attention and/or the urgency of the issues they face, and such pressure can lead to erroneous choices from a long-term perspective, such as when key implementation difficulties or budget implications are not anticipated correctly in the rush to adopt a bill before a legislative deadline. Public managers, through the agencies they serve, can help to foster the development of policy ideas long before these issues reach the policy agenda, so that critical shortcomings have been more fully anticipated and corresponding remedial measures prepared to be put in place. Public managers can also help to ensure that recognition of these policy issues is followed up in later stages of the policy-making process, as the attention of both the policy-makers and the public to a particular issue may dwindle as new issues emerge.

3. *Decision-making.* Decision-making involves officially sanctioned or authorized individuals, or groups, deciding to adopt a particular course of action for implementation. Public managers can be involved in decision-making in various capacities, depending on their rank and the type of organization in which they work. Senior-level public managers often share the responsibility for making policy decisions with the political leaders they serve. Public managers in charge of policy development and planning divisions, or departments, at various levels of government are also often asked to make policy recommendations for key decisions, and their expertise on specific policy issues enables them to have a significant

say in decision-making because of the complexity of contemporary public problems. Public managers at relatively lower levels in the administrative ladder can also play a significant role in shaping decisions by providing useful insights about administrative feasibility, a critical criterion for decision-making.

4. *Policy implementation.* Implementation is a key activity in the policy process in which a policy is given form and effect. While the central importance of public managers in policy implementation is widely recognized, the potential of public managers to improve policy outcomes is often far from fully realized. The reoccurring and omnipresent inconsistencies between policy design and implementation suggest much improvement can be made through creative and discerning efforts by public managers. Policies decided in the political arena are often broad and vague, leaving crucial details to public officials to work out. In addition, the fact that public managers (and the agencies they serve) are provided with mandates to carry out certain policies does not mean that the resources needed for implementation, and support from key stakeholders, are guaranteed. To be effective, public managers need to develop expertise and policy acumen in networking, advocating, and negotiation, a set of functions that are often relatively unfamiliar to them if they have been trained in the classic mode of public administration focussing on hierarchical chains of accountability, and responsibility to superiors and political executives.

5. *Policy evaluation.* Policy evaluation is a critical policy activity in that it involves the assessment of the extent to which a public policy is achieving its stated objectives and, if not, what can be done to improve it. Their direct access to information on policy performance provides distinct advantages to public managers over other key players in this set of activities, and potentially offers them many opportunities to engage in different policy-making tasks, such as agenda setting and policy formulation, tied to policy reform and alteration. However, such potential, again, has been largely untapped, in part due to many public managers' fears of being undermined by negative evaluations of their work, but also often due to a lack of expertise in the technical aspects of evaluation on their part.

Policy perspectives

The second layer concerns the perspectives that public managers need to adopt in approaching their roles in the policy process. To realize the full potential of their roles in contemporary governmental policy-making, public managers need to simultaneously take three perspectives to guide their participation in the policy process: organizational, political, and technical. The effectiveness of public managers' policy roles will be undermined if any of the perspectives is ignored or not adequately dealt with. While the significance of the three dimensions will differ considerably across levels of government and policy sectors, they are always vital to varying degrees.

1. *Organizational perspective.* The organizational perspective focusses public managers' attention to organizational issues—such as organizational design, organizational changes, management of human and financial resources, and administrative procedure—required to respond to the challenges they face in the policy process. The organizational perspective requires public managers to think beyond their managerial roles in their own organizations by focussing on challenges and opportunities brought about by the broader institutional context of policy development.

2. *Technical perspective.* The technical perspective focusses public managers' attention on the utilitarian objective held highly in public policy—the greatest benefits for largest number of people—requiring them to think analytically and systematically about the causes and consequences of policy issues as well as the likely outcomes of the various policy options available to tackle them. Notwithstanding the widespread perception that public servants are technical experts in the area in which they work, they often lack even general training in public policy analysis and management, much less training in analysing and managing the sector in which they work. The immense uncertainties and complexities that characterize the policy world aggravates their limitations in technical matters but must be overcome in order to promote better policies and policy outcomes.

3. *Political perspective.* The politics of public policy is about who gets what through the policy process, and public managers need to understand the political world if they are to be successful. They need to be particularly in tune with the political dynamics underlying the policy activities in which they engage. Identifying the key actors and understanding their essential interests and ideologies, as well as the relationships among them, are essential traits of successful public managers. So is an understanding of the political trade-offs necessary for securing an agreement among contending actors and interests on a particular course of action.

Policy competencies

The third layer in the framework focusses on the capacities of public managers to effectively participate in the five policy-making functions. In order to do so they require a set of administrative competencies including policy acumen, analytical skills, and managerial expertise.

1. *Policy acumen.* Policy acumen consists of the accumulated knowledge and experience in the policy process, including understanding of the key players, their key interests and their strategies and resources. It also includes a broad understanding of the policy practices of other countries and/or different policy sectors. This knowledge and experience forms a solid basis for judgment about policy feasibility: what will work and what will not. Public managers are often particularly weak in the development of policy acumen due to lack of training in public policy as well as lack of experience in actively participating in the policy process or familiarity with other country or sector experiences.

2. *Analytical skills.* The second capacity necessary for effectively participating in the policy process is analytical skills for diagnosing a situation and developing appropriate strategies. For example, analytical tools such as political mapping and stakeholder analysis enable public managers to assess the support for existing and proposed policy measures, while cost-benefit analysis and other similar techniques help them to compare the consequences and costs of various options available. While not all public managers may be directly involved in conducting the different forms of analysis, instead depending on their professional and organizational colleagues, it is critical for them to be familiar with their potential, and the limitations of the various analytical tools, in order to be intelligent consumers of analyses produced by others.

3. *Managerial expertise.* Public managers' capacities to perform key managerial functions—such as planning, organizing, staffing, directing, and controlling—also significantly shapes their ability to participate effectively in the policy process. For example, managerial expertise may allow public managers to exert greater influence in agenda setting where their efforts in sustaining attention to key public issues are critical. In addition, their managerial expertise may provide opportunities to lead the development of alternative forms of network management or better coordinate and direct the activities of a multitude of actors who might be involved in policy formulation, implementation or other policy functions.

2 Agenda setting

Agenda setting concerns the process by which governments decide which issues need their attention. It focusses on, among other things, the determination and definition of what constitutes the "problem" that subsequent policy actions are intended to resolve. The reasons why governments often fail to respond to public issues to the satisfaction of their citizens can often be traced back to two fundamental defects, both of which originate in agenda setting:

1. many critical public problems fail to reach official policy agendas, while many relatively minor concerns do; and
2. the poor framing of public problems leads to preoccupation with ineffective and/or wasteful solutions that preclude consideration of alternative solutions with the potential to resolve the problem.

Public managers are well positioned to tackle these and other defects in agenda setting and thus improve policy processes and outcomes. However, in reality, this potential remains largely untapped for a variety of reasons, including the widespread perception that their responsibility is confined to administrative and organizational tasks, to the exclusion of the political and technical considerations that characterize agenda setting. In this chapter we present various opportunities, circumstances, and strategies that public managers can employ to play a meaningful role in agenda-setting.

The basics of agenda setting

What is agenda setting?

An agenda is a list of issues or problems to which governmental officials and others in the policy community are paying some serious attention at any given time. Agenda setting is about a government recognizing that a problem is a "public" problem worthy of its attention (and not simply an issue affecting only a few a people, or a background "condition" about which it can do very little and so one that should rather be endured). Agenda setting is concerned with the initial processes of issue identification and policy initiation and with the manner in which these processes affect subsequent policy-making activities undertaken by governments. Agenda items differ greatly, depending on the nature of the economic and social circumstances in which people live and governments operate. In China, for example, the government's top agenda in the first decade of the twenty-first century included food prices, food safety, growing air pollution, and the 2008 Beijing Olympics. In France, on the other hand, priorities included the reform of the pension system for public sector employees, the quality of the education system, and immigration.

Agenda setting is sometimes defined as the process by which the demands of various groups in the population are translated into items that governments consider for action. This definition is closely linked with the idea that public policy-making is driven primarily by the actions of nongovernmental actors to which government managers react. Empirical evidence, however, has shown that in many instances concerns about certain policy problems are in fact raised by members of governments rather than social groups. In either case, however, public managers must understand how demands for policy action can arise and are placed on the formal agenda of government.

Agenda setting is characterized by three key features. It is a process that:

1. is nonlinear,
2. is political as well as technical, and
3. takes place within a complex network of state and societal actors.

Public managers need to understand these three characteristics if they are to respond appropriately to the social and political concerns raised by their constituents and clients. They must also understand:

1. the material interests of both social and state actors in relation to any particular issue,
2. the institutional and ideological contexts in which they operate, and
3. the potential for change in the contingent circumstances that shape discussions and debates on public issues.

Main actors in agenda setting

Actors participating in agenda setting include both state and societal actors operating at subnational, national, and international levels. Many key actors in the agenda-setting process are state actors, including elected officials as well as appointed administrators. Elected officials include legislators and executive members, while appointees include bureaucrats and members of the judiciary. Each has the legal authority to bring items to the attention of government for further action and thus plays a key role in agenda setting activity.

The range of societal actors involved in this process is much larger, and potentially limitless, since it is sometimes possible for individuals, acting as activists, litigants, or voters, to bring items to the government agenda. However, it is more common for agenda items to emerge from organized "collective" actors, such as interest groups, religious organizations, companies, labor unions, associations, think tanks, or other kinds of policy research organizations. These actors command different kinds of resources, from economic power to knowledge, which give them different levels of ability to influence government thinking and attention on various issues or aspects of issues. Among interest groups, business is generally the most powerful, with an unmatched capacity for affecting public policy through its direct control over investment and, hence, indirectly, over jobs and economic prosperity. Labor too occupies a powerful position among social groups in countries with high unionization rates, though it is typically less powerful than business, on whom it relies for job creation and wages.

Surprising as it may appear, "the public" often plays a rather small and only indirect role in the public policy process. This is not to say that its role is inconsequential, as it provides the backdrop of norms, attitudes, and values against which the policy process unfolds. However, in most liberal democracies, rather than the citizens themselves, it is their representatives who are entrusted with the task of governing. But insofar as these representatives depend on their appeal to voters in order to win elections, they need to take public opinion into account. And elections provide platforms for political parties to organize the election efforts of politicians to control legislative and executive offices. Once in existence, parties work to put innovative strategies forward in order to win elections, including preparation of policy packages to appeal to voters. These packages often form a vital source of public policy agendas, which public managers must be prepared to address after the election.

Another significant set of societal actors in the policy process is made up of researchers working at universities, research institutes, and think tanks. These organizations maintain an interest in a broad range of policy problems and use their expertise to enable them to develop a comprehensive perspective on the issues facing governments. Their research tends to be directed at proposing practical solutions for public problems or, in the case of some think tanks, finding evidence to support the ideologically driven positions they advocate on behalf of those who fund them. This sets them apart somewhat from academic researchers at universities and research organizations who tend to have broader interests and do not necessarily seek to find or advocate practical solutions for policy problems. Explicitly partisan research is also generally eschewed in academia.

In societies with a relatively free press, the media can also play an important role in bringing issues onto the public and government agendas. The development of information and communication technologies has greatly empowered the media to shape public opinion on public problems. Their ability to name and blame a policy for a problem can sometimes force an issue onto the agenda. The extensive reporting of the health implications of smoking, for example, heavily influenced the antismoking legislation passed in a number of countries. However, this does not mean that the media directly controls agenda setting and other policy processes. Often, the media itself suffers from a lack of access to information, poor reporting, and a host of other factors that limit their ability to set government agendas.

International actors play an increasingly significant role in policy agenda setting. These actors may be individuals working as advisers or consultants to national governments or donor organizations, or members of international organizations with the authority under international agreements to regulate their members' behavior. International actors are likely to find it easier to intervene in policy sectors in which there is an international agreement sanctioning their intervention. The central place occupied by the International Monetary Fund (IMF) in the international monetary regime, for example, enables its officers to interfere in the details of public policy-making in many nations facing serious financial or fiscal problems. An even more significant resource is the possession of theoretical and practical expertise in a policy sector. Many international organizations—for example, the United Nations, World Bank, International Monetary Fund (IMF), World Health Organization (WHO)—are repositories of immense expertise in policy issues with the result that national governments often rely upon them when making policies, thus giving them significant influence in domestic policy processes. The financial resources that international organizations can dispense to governments form another source of influence that can help move specific items, or specific approaches to certain problems, onto government agendas.

Initiation of agenda setting

The demands for government action can come from both inside and outside governments. These processes can be described as *inside initiation* and *outside initiation* respectively. In the case of *inside initiation*, the government controls almost every aspect of problem definition and issue articulation. In such cases, government officials can often place an issue onto the formal agenda of government even in the absence of a publicly recognized grievance. There may be considerable debate within a government over the issue, but the public may well be unaware of the policy and its development until its formal announcement. Inside initiation also includes situations when influential groups with special access to the government initiate a policy without the general public's involvement. The wish to exclude public scrutiny may be a result of technical as well as political reasons, for example when it is feared that an issue might be hijacked or stalled by opponents. International lending agencies, for example, have been alleged to have initiated in unpopular policy reforms in this manner.

In the case of *outside initiation*, issues appear on the government agenda as a result of "pressure" from individuals, groups, and organizations outside government. Issues arise in a nongovernmental area and are then expanded sufficiently to reach, first, the public or informal agenda and then the formal or government agenda. Outside actors encounter more difficulty in seizing control of the agenda than their government counterparts but can do so through various kinds of public issue campaigns as well as insider lobbying. This can occur through a range of activities, from organizing letter-writing or media campaigns to picketing and civil disobedience.

The formal agenda of government and the informal public agenda are not independent of each other. Government activities such as public education and information campaigns, as well as more direct measures such as specific public works projects or expenditure plans, have an effect on the kinds of issues defined by the public as "problems," providing a kind of "feedback" loop between government action and public problem perception and definition. These highlight the complex relationships existing between the formal agenda of the government and the informal public agenda, which must be understood by public managers if they are to achieve their policy goals.

Policy communities, which consist of a specific set of actors involved in defining and interpreting a problem and identifying solutions to it, often play a significant role in bridging the formal and informal agenda. The "image" a policy problem has within a policy community—that is, how it is named, claimed, blamed, and framed by different policy actors—influences a problem's articulation, deliberation, and resolution. Hence, when a problem such as unemployment, for example, is portrayed as a technical economic issue rather than a social one, economic experts may dominate policy-making and solutions can be discussed within a frame of immigration targets, apprenticeship quotas, or tax burdens. When the ethical, social, or political aspects of the problem assume the center stage, however, a much broader range of participants might be involved, as happens when unemployment is defined as a result of the unequal distribution of income, wealth, or opportunities.

Framing and agenda setting

There are multiple ways to frame a particular policy in a given context, and the ways in which problems are defined and (re)framed dictates how they are treated in subsequent policy activities. For example, if the problem of the low school enrolment rate for girls in many countries is defined merely as an education problem, it might not receive adequate attention from a government. But if it is framed as a developmental problem affecting a population's health, housing, labor productivity, economic growth, and poverty, it may receive a rather different reaction and a higher priority, motivating swifter public investment in female education. Public managers can encourage the framing of problems in ways that expand the constituency in support of their prioritization and, ultimately, resolution. Government-sponsored activities such as education and information campaigns, for example, can affect the kinds of issues perceived by the public as problems and how they are perceived.

Both state and non-state actors attempt to construct "policy monopolies" that control the definition and image of a problem. A loss of agenda control by state actors, however, can happen when contextual scans are poor or not performed, allowing other state and societal actors to rally support for their own naming and framing of issues. This was the case, for example, when the issue of U.S. involvement in war in the Middle East was framed by the U.S. media in 2006 not as "how to achieve victory," but "how to cut losses," and not "whether" to withdraw troops but "when." A sudden crisis may foist a problem on the public agenda and help to break down an existing image "monopoly," allowing different views of policy problems and solutions to compete in public and government discourses.

Policy windows and agenda setting

Timing is critical in agenda setting. The concept of a "policy window" or "opportunity opening" through which an issue may be placed onto a government agenda drives home the point that the agenda-setting process is sometimes governed by fortuitous happenings that can force problems to the forefront. This can happen, for example, when an airliner crashes and forces changes to safety practices, or when an election produces an unexpected turnover in key decision-makers and brings a new set of policy issues associated with the winner onto the policy agenda.

Potentially, four types of policy windows exist. Public managers need to be aware of these different opportunities for agenda entrance and be prepared to take advantage of them when they occur:

- *routinized windows*: in which routinized procedural events such as budget cycles dictate window openings;
- *discretionary windows*: where individual political behavior on the part of decision-makers dictates window openings;
- *random windows*: where unforeseen events, such as disasters or scandals, open windows; and
- *spill-over windows*: where related issues are drawn into already opened windows in other sectors or issue areas, such as when railway safety issues arise due to the increased attention paid to airline or automobile safety due to some crisis or accident.

In order to be ready to take advantage of opportunities presented to develop options consistent with their goals, public managers must have the capacity to identify and act upon the specific circumstances present or likely to be present in their areas of interest. Most policy windows, in fact, open quite predictably. Legislation comes up for renewal on schedule, for instance, creating opportunities to change, expand, or abolish certain programs.

However, regardless of their source, open windows are scarce and often short-lived. Opportunities come, but they also pass. Windows do not stay open long. If a chance is missed, another must be awaited, sometimes for a very long time. The strategies of agenda control that public managers employ, then, should include the ability to prepare for the different kinds of windows that may open, often despite a lack of analytical capacity to predict and prepare for them.

Challenges in agenda setting

Agenda setting is often considered to be the most critical stage in policy process, since without it there would be no policy to speak of, but it is probably also the least well understood of all the stages in the policy process. It is critical to understand that not all public problems are acknowledged as problems by governments, and because of their resource and time constraints, there are only a limited number of public problems on the policy agenda that governments can address at any particular time.

This means there is a good chance of a public problem prioritized on the public agenda failing to correspond to its relative importance on the government agenda. In fact the process by which different policy problems vying for the attention of policy-makers are sorted out and defined is highly complex, adding to the challenges faced by public managers in directing or controlling policy agendas.

The challenges confronting public managers in agenda setting are numerous, and only some of the more significant among them are noted here.

First, the policy agenda is often dominated by demands for responses to crises, but due to the pressure and short timescale associated with them, governments are often forced to take some easily available course of action, which can increase the risks of making poor decisions leading to poor outcomes. Unfortunately, this pattern of crisis-driven agendas is very difficult to avoid and requires both a high level of policy capacity on the part of administrators as well as a great deal of autonomy from public pressures for quick action. Such factors are often in very short supply in many governments.

A second, and closely related, phenomenon is that, until a crisis breaks out, a public problem may struggle to be placed onto policy agendas. However, often the costs of dealing with a crisis are much higher than would be the case if pre-emptive measures had been taken to prevent its occurrence. A good example of this can be seen in the failure of many African countries to deal with HIV/AIDS through preventive programs until the disease was already widespread and ravaging their populations.

Third, agenda setting is sometimes used as a means for politicians to pay lip-service to policy problems in order to score political points rather than make genuine efforts to address genuine problems. This is the case in many countries, for example, with the phenomenon of homelessness, which many politicians claim is a major concern while continuing to fail to develop realistic plans or processes to deal with it.

Fourth, governments often tend to define problems in ways that absolve them of the responsibility for causing or aggravating a problem and/or whose resolution involves the least effort on their part. While this may benefit the government, it misdirects policy efforts and will eventually lead to the problem remaining unresolved. The well-known tendency of many governments to "blame the victim" in various criminal or health circumstances, for example, allows them to avoid responsibility for improving physical or social security.

Fifth, "overcrowding" of the policy agenda is a pervasive problem in agenda setting. At its root lies the reluctance of many politicians to say "no" to the inclusion of specific group problems on government agendas because of pressure from their constituencies and special interest groups. The result is the inclusion of too many problems on the policy agenda when there are neither the resources nor the time to deal with them effectively, which in turn diffuses the limited resources that might have been used to deal with a smaller agenda more effectively.

Finally, agenda setting may be hijacked by the media and/or special interest groups with little concern for overall government, social priorities, or the connections of specific problems to others. For example, in many countries in recent decades business has been particularly adept at defining social policy problems as issues that need to be considered in conjunction with the need to attract foreign investment, thus promoting market solutions and affecting how basic services such as water and transportation are delivered to the population, regardless of how these services might be best delivered in particular circumstances.

Regardless of how it occurs, poor framing of public problems often leads to the persistence of ineffective and/or wasteful "solutions" to them. And, if governments prioritize the wrong policy issues, the chances of developing good policies may be missed from the very beginning, despite the efforts that might be made in subsequent stages of the policy process.

Strategies for public managers in agenda setting

Public managers are well placed to deal with all of the challenges mentioned above. First, where they enjoy professional status as career public servants, they are able to have substantial impacts in *sustaining* the attention, or intensity of it, on particular policy issues over a long period of time. Second, due to their expertise and experience, public managers may be well positioned to identify changing social needs in the policy environment. They may also serve as a *reality check* (or fact verifiers) both for policy ideas coming from the top and for issues pushed by societal actors, "screening" them in terms of cost and feasibility. Third, their control over access to information with regard to the outcomes of existing policies and programs provides public managers with a unique channel to shape policy priorities. Finally, public managers, as prominent actors in the policy process, can ensure that various channels for policy issues to reach policy agendas, both internal and external to government, coexist and complement each other.

On the other hand, public managers also face obstacles that impede their role in agenda setting. First, they may lack legitimacy in agenda setting if their role is defined too narrowly (such as implementation only). Second, they may have little room to maneuver if there is tight control over their budgets, information, and activities. Third, most public managers lack the communication, persuasion, and negotiation skills essential for effective engagement with politicians and the public in agenda setting. Fourth, they may occupy a marginal position within a policy community and experience difficulty working across organizational or sectoral boundaries to confront complex problems. Finally, they may lack the analytical capacity—skills, resources, and necessary information—required for the accurate diagnosis of policy problems.

Leveraging on their positions and resources to shape issue definition

There are many ways to define (frame) a policy problem and indeed *how* the problem is defined will usually shape what is done about it. Public managers can employ their experience and expertise to map their environment, assess the implications of different actor interpretations, and channel their efforts toward ensuring that more feasible interpretations prevail. The causes of a problem as expressed by the public, the media, or politicians may be very different from their actual root causes: public managers can use data and theoretical frameworks (such as the analysis of market failures or government failures, for example) to guide the search for sound, empirically valid, or "evidence-based" problem definition.

While governments usually try to control the formal policy agenda, the fact that this agenda is inextricably linked to the larger social agenda of perceived problems means that it is easy for a government to lose control of its own agenda and find itself reacting to an almost random set of concerns and issues raised by the population. This must be avoided because careful sequencing of issues and solutions is required if effective, integrated policy-making is to take place. Governmental actors are able to play a major role in issue naming, blaming, claiming, and framing; either informally through their contacts with societal actors, or formally through their influence over the media, think tanks, or academics. In this way they can influence the direction of policy-making at the agenda-setting stage by naming and framing an issue in such a way as to promote, authenticate, or legitimize the claims and blames of specific sets of policy actors.

In many instances of outside initiation, for example, public managers within the government may feel that they have little control over the issues they address because problems are defined outside of the government. But this is not to say that public managers cannot influence the definition of a problem or the types of proposed solutions, only that they may not be able to control the timing of an issue's emergence. To succeed, however, outside initiators must have the requisite political resources and skills to outmaneuver their opponents or advocates of other issues and actions. And this provides an opportunity for public managers to affect their behavior.

In the case of society-driven initiation, social actors need to be able to access the most relevant information. Public managers can facilitate some initiators' articulation of issues and concerns, for example, by providing information on substantive issues or governmental processes that can help outside policy initiators navigate complex routes onto the official government agenda. Public managers can also help secure such access by organizing or institutionalizing stakeholder consultations and other forms of participatory policy-making. The public managers can work to involve both those actors that are intimately involved in project or policy proposals ("insiders") and those likely to be involved at some point in the future ("outsiders").

Such consultative processes typically include both short-term and long-term mechanisms to provide recommendations to the government concerning policy problems. Advisory committees, commissions, task forces, and roundtables, for example, are all forms of government-appointed bodies for developing problem definitions acceptable to both social and state actors, who will then have a better chance to successfully negotiate the remaining stages of the policy process. The appointment of members of the public to these and other institutional bodies is, in itself, a means of increasing the representation of unorganized public interests, both at the agenda-setting stage and throughout the entire policy process.

In *inside* initiation, public managers enjoy more leeway in defining and redefining policy problems and searching for solutions than is the case for *outside* initiation, and they are also better able to control the timing of an issue's emergence as well as the ways in which it proceeds into official policy-making procedures. This greatly aids their ability to integrate demands and concerns into bundles of integrated policies.

In some cases, for example, there may be considerable debate within government over an issue such as climate change mitigation, but the public may well be kept in the dark about the policy and its development until its formal announcement. The policy may be specified in some detail or it may indicate only general principles whose specification will be worked out later. While some public managers may feel that a secretive process would avoid lengthy delays, however it may be desirable to be more transparent in order to increase support for the new policy, as successful implementation often depends on a favorable public reaction. This is very much the case with solutions that might require either an attitudinal or organizational change on the part of members of the public. In such cases, public managers can ensure that government leaders hold meetings and engage in public relations campaigns aimed at mobilizing public support for their decisions. Reform of the pension system for public sector employees in France or alteration to the subsidies paid to Greek or Polish farmers, for example, may be initiated from within the government, but cannot move forward without adequate mobilization efforts.

Managing agenda entrance strategically

As discussed above, public managers must be able to identify and manage the different types of windows that lead to agenda entrance. Routinized windows, for example, are very important and are the most common opportunity to raise a substantive policy issue. Every political and administrative system has its own annual cycles and rhythms—for example, "Speeches from the Throne" or "State of the Union" addresses, or annual or semi-annual legislative tabling of budget estimates—that act as opportunities for the consideration of new policy initiatives and the (re)evaluation of ongoing ones. Astute managers must make themselves aware of these cycles and related internal deadlines and plan ahead to ensure that their problems are promoted in these opportunities.

Most "discretionary" windows are also not random and can also be managed, if not always predicted. That is, while "random" matters sometimes reach the agenda as a result of a pressing problem or "focussing event," such as a scandal or emergency crisis, such events and problems almost always need the accompaniment or preparation of potential policy solutions, which public managers can provide. Crises, disasters, symbols, and other focussing events only rarely carry a subject to policy agenda prominence by themselves. They need to be accompanied by both political support and an available solution, and usually succeed only when they reinforce some pre-existing perception of a problem. Astute managers, again, will be prepared for such opportunities through forward planning by having prepared alternatives ready to be unveiled when a crisis or discretionary opportunity arises.

Although it is sometimes felt by public managers that they can create their own windows, this is rarely the case. Sometimes formal government agendas can be jammed to overflowing by extensive budgetary and housekeeping responsibilities, by fundamental revision of established polices, and by pressing problems from various crises. During such periods governments are engaged mainly in reacting to the demands of outside political forces and are able to exercise little choice in the establishment of their own agendas. Much time and effort can be wasted by public managers in attempting to promote the opening of a policy window when they would have been better advised to wait for either an institutional window or a crisis window to open, which they could take advantage of.

The extent to which institutional procedures allow, promote, or prevent the occurrence of entrepreneurial political activity by public managers is a significant factor in determining the propensity for predictable and unpredictable windows to occur. Where time allocation in legislative institutions, for example, remains largely in the hands of government—as in parliamentary systems—the opportunities for discretionary agenda setting are highly restricted. Where time allocation is somewhat more flexible—as in countries with presidential political systems—the opportunities for individual policy initiatives is much greater. Public managers should be aware of these differences in political regimes, and their consequences for the timing of agenda initiatives, and plan their activities accordingly.

Forming strategic alliances with non-state actors

Public managers can establish strategic alliances with non-state actors through regular consultations with key stakeholders in order to enhance their effectiveness in agenda setting. Consultations strengthen their legitimacy and hence effectiveness. Consultation with stakeholders may be organized so as to facilitate articulation and aggregation of public grievances.

Cooperation among different policy initiators outside the government is often required if an issue is to successfully proceed through to the governmental agenda and beyond. If this cooperation is not forthcoming, or the goals of the government and societal groups are too diffuse, the government might have to neutralize or co-opt certain groups in order to move forward what it believes to be an important agenda item. If this cooperation is not readily forthcoming, achieving the support required for government action can require a wider range of government efforts, such as public information or education campaigns, or the provision of subsidies and other kinds of incentives. While the merits of such actions can prove beneficial in educating the public and encouraging it to support government actions, it can also dramatically slow down the speed of policy-making and render its outcomes very uncertain. It can, for example, allow other groups to mobilize and advocate alternative conceptions of policy problems and solutions, or demand the withdrawal of an item from the government agenda. Public managers are, therefore, well advised to "get out in front" of an issue and facilitate the convergence of views among different social groups rather than reactively attempting to "divide and conquer" their opposition once they are already active.

In most market economies public managers must also recognize that industries and businesses tend to have unique influences on agenda setting. As such, close attention must be paid to these actors and their interests. Public managers in industrial and business sectors, however, should also reach out to other groups and actors, such as consumer associations and environmental groups, when seeking to steer the agenda-setting process toward integration. Voluntary sector organizations can also be mobilized through, for example, the extension of funding to them for service delivery or for policy monitoring purposes. Such funds increase their organizational resources, which can also be applied to their naming, claiming, blaming, and framing agenda-setting activities.

Encouraging public participation is a key method of state-led agenda setting that can trigger mobilization, stimulate "outside initiation," or build support for and legitimize an "inside-initiation" process. Such processes can range from relatively passive public hearings and opinion polling (requiring only a response to a political survey) to the attendance of the representatives of political parties, interest groups, or other individuals at formal hearings.

As mentioned above, a key technique available to public managers seeking to control the agenda-setting process is the creation of consultative bodies of various kinds—for example, boards, commissions, and tribunals. These bodies can provide an institutionalized means for involving non-governmental actors in the agenda-setting processes and a mechanism for the development of problem definitions that are acceptable to both social and state actors, and hence that are likely to successfully negotiate the remaining stages of the policy process.

Without such efforts, public managers may find themselves reluctantly reacting to an almost random set of disparate and randomly occurring concerns and issues raised by various members of the public. Governments, however, should not just leave agenda setting to social actors, because they have a clear responsibility to govern and provide leadership on public issues.

Conclusion

Agenda setting is where public policy starts. Unless a problem gets onto the government's agenda, nothing will be done about it. How a problem comes to be viewed as a problem involves complex social and political processes as well as changing circumstances, such as the emergence of a crisis, and these complicate public managers' roles in agenda setting. If they are not to be overwhelmed by these factors, public managers need a sound knowledge base, strong analytical skills, and a well-crafted but flexible strategy. This chapter has offered some pointers in this direction.

The inclusion of a problem in the government's policy agenda is, however, only a start. It needs to go through two more stages—policy formulation and decision-making—before the government will actually start doing something concrete about the problem. We now turn to policy formulation.

Further reading

Anderson, George (1996) "The New Focus on the Policy Capacity of the Federal Government" *Canadian Public Administration* 39(4): 469–88.

Bakvis, H. (1997) "Advising the Executive: Think Tanks, Consultants, Political Staff and Kitchen Cabinets" in P. Weller, H. Bakvis, and R. A. W. Rhodes (Eds.), *The Hollow Crown: Countervailing Trends in Core Executives*. New York: St. Martin's Press, pp. 84–125.

Baumgartner, F. R. and B. D. Jones (1991) "Agenda Dynamics and Policy Subsystems" *Journal of Politics* 53(4): 1044–74.

Binderkrantz, A. (2005) "Interest Group Strategies: Navigating between Privileged Access and Strategies of Pressure" *Political Studies* 53: 694–715.

Birkland, T. A. (2004) "'The World Changed Today': Agenda-Setting and Policy Change in the Wake of the September 11 Terrorist Attacks" *Review of Policy Research* 21(2): 179–200.

—— (1998) "Focusing Events, Mobilization, and Agenda-Setting" *Journal of Public Policy* 18(1): 53–74.

Cobb, R. W. and C. D. Elder (1972) *Participation in American Politics: The Dynamics of Agenda-Building*. Boston, MA: Allyn & Bacon.

Cobb, R., J. K. Ross, and M. H. Ross (1976) "Agenda Building as a Comparative Political Process" *American Political Science Review* 70(1): 126–38.

Cobb, R. W. and M. H. Ross (Eds.) (1997) *Cultural Strategies of Agenda Denial: Avoidance, Attack and Redefinition*. Lawrence, KS: University Press of Kansas.

Colebatch, H. K. and B. A. Radin (2006) "Mapping the Work of Policy" in H. K. Colebatch (Ed.), *The Work of Policy: An International Survey*. New York: Rowman & Littlefield, pp. 217–26.

Dery, D. (2000) "Agenda-Setting and Problem Definition" *Policy Studies* 21(1): 37–47.

Dion, L. (1973) "The Politics of Consultation" *Government and Opposition* 8(3): 332–53.

Erbring, L. and E. N. Goldenberg (1980) "Front Page News and Real World Cues: A New Look at Agenda-Setting by the Media" *American Journal of Political Science* 24(1): 16–49.

Felstiner, W. L. F., R. L. Abeland, and A. Sarat (1980) "The Emergence and Transformation of Disputes: Naming, Blaming, Claiming" *Law and Society Review* 15(3–4): 631–54.

Fischer, F. (2003) *Reframing Public Policy: Discursive Politics and Deliberative Practices*. Oxford: Oxford University Press.

Hammond, T. H. (1986) "Agenda Control, Organizational Structure, and Bureaucratic Politics" *American Journal of Political Science* 30(2): 379–420.

Hansford, T. G. (2004) "Lobbying Strategies, Venue Selection, and Organized Interest Involvement at the U.S. Supreme Court" *American Politics Research* 32(2): 170–97.

Howlett, M. (1998) "Predictable and Unpredictable Policy Windows: Issue, Institutional and Exogenous Correlates of Canadian Federal Agenda-Setting" *Canadian Journal of Political Science* 31(3): 495–524.

Jones, B. D. (1994) *Re-Conceiving Decision-Making in Democratic Politics: Attention, Choice and Public Policy*. Chicago, IL: University of Chicago Press.

Kingdon, J. W. (1984) *Agendas, Alternatives, and Public Policies*. Boston, MA: Little Brown & Company.

Montpetit, E. (2003) "Public Consultations in Policy Network Environments" *Canadian Public Policy* 29(1): 95–110.

Painter, M. and J. Pierre (2005) *Challenges to State Policy Capacity: Global Trends and Comparative Perspectives*. London: Palgrave Macmillan.

Peters, B. G. (1996) *The Policy Capacity of Government*. Ottawa: Canadian Centre for Management Development.

Pierre, J. (1998) "Public Consultation and Citizen Participation: Dilemmas of Policy Advice" in B. G. Peters and D. J. Savoie (Eds.), *Taking Stock: Assessing Public Sector Reforms*. Montreal, QC, Canada: McGill-Queen's Press, pp. 137–63.

Pritchard, D. (1992) *The News Media and Public Policy Agendas. Public Opinion, the Press, and Public Policy* in J. D. Kennamer (Ed.), Westport, CT: Praeger, pp. 103–12.

Rochefort, D. A. and R. W. Cobb (1993) "Problem Definition, Agenda Access, and Policy Choice" *Policy Studies Journal* 21(1): 56–71.

Rochefort, D. A. and R. W. Cobb (1994). *The Politics of Problem Definition: Shaping the Policy Agenda*. Lawrence, KS: University of Kansas Press.

Smith, T. B. (1977) "Advisory Committees in the Public Policy Process" *International Review of Administrative Sciences* 43(2): 153–66.

Stone, D. A. (1989) "Causal Stories and the Formation of Policy Agendas" *Political Science Quarterly* 104(2): 281–300.

3 Policy formulation

The commitment of governments in tackling the prevalent policy problems facing many countries, such as corruption, environmental degradation, and poverty, is often admirably strong. However, converting such commitment to measurable achievements requires the development of a set of policy options that can meet three conditions simultaneously: they must be politically acceptable, administratively feasible, and technically sound. The persistence (or worsening) of problems in many countries, unfortunately, suggests that the ability of existing policy processes to generate such policy options cannot be taken for granted. Too often, policy-makers are pressured to choose from three unappealing choices: policy options suffering noticeable deficiencies, policy options only marginally differing from existing policies, and undertaking no action at all.

This chapter provides an overview of the challenges public managers confront in generating better policy options. It addresses the roles they play in formulation, the constraints they face, and the strategies they can adopt to enhance their effectiveness. We first define the essential features and imperatives of policy formulation. We next discuss why and how public managers need to participate effectively in this activity. The last two sections discuss the obstacles to coherent policy formulation and how they may be overcome by concerted efforts on the part of public managers.

The basics of policy formulation

What is policy formulation?

Policy formulation refers to the process of generating a set of plausible policy choices for addressing problems. At this stage of the policy process, a range of potential policy choices is identified and a preliminary assessment of their feasibility is offered.

It is critical to point out that policy formulation as conceptualized here is different from what is described in more linear depictions of the policy process, which tend to restrict formulation activities to those that start only after a policy problem has entered onto a formal policy agenda and end after a range of options has been identified. Policy formulation, as we use the term here, extends throughout the policy process. The search for new policy options thus may precede the initiation of a policy problem in agenda setting and may extend beyond the point where a decision is made and implemented, to the evaluation of existing and future potential means to resolve public problems.

It is precisely in this larger overall context where public managers can be expected to have the greatest impact on the generation of policy options. Their presence at most stages of the policy process provides them with many opportunities to integrate the search and selection of policy options with other stages of policy-making. Their longevity in their jobs can help ensure that the search for improvements through the creation, adoption, and diffusion of new policy options is sustained and cumulative in nature.

Actors in policy formulation

Exactly who is involved in policy formulation in any given policy-making circumstance depends on the nature of the overall political system as well as the concrete characteristics of the policy in question. However, it is possible to offer some generalizations.

Policy formulation often conveys an image of some high-level activity carried out by a small group of senior officials (both appointed and elected) and there is some truth in this characterization. The political executives (cabinet ministers in parliamentary systems and departmental secretaries in presidential systems) are often the most prominent and publicly visible figures involved in policy formulation, especially on high-profile issues. Their involvement takes different forms, for example leading key government agencies or participating in presidential commissions, task forces, and high-level interagency committees. While the positions they occupy typically require them to take a more holistic view of policy options than administrators, in practice they are often restricted in the kinds of solutions they might consider by political imperatives (such as a government's re-election prospects or existing ideological and political mandates).

Legislators are also often involved in policy formulation, either through the development of new legislation or, more commonly, through conducting both a legislative overview and a legislative review. While collectively they are constrained by the expectation that they represent the preferences of their constituents and the public, individually they are also constrained by their party's policy stances and their own personal political ambitions.

The key government agencies in the policy sector in question, however, are typically the most common main actors in policy formulation. Most policy options available for application to a problem are first developed in government agencies, which typically have considerable cumulative knowledge and expertise in a particular policy area. While their vast experience is an asset, however, the same experience is also sometimes a barrier to "thinking outside the box" and the formulation of new, creative options for dealing with existing or new problems. Government officials also can find it difficult to take a holistic view beyond their own or their agency's routine tasks and existing policy tools, and they may be less than enthusiastic about policy alternatives involving significant changes to the status quo.

While a great deal of attention has been paid to the role of senior officials, often in central agencies or attached to ministers' offices, in proposing policy alternatives, mid-level managers also play an often hidden but equally vital role in the process, albeit in support of their superiors. They need to take this responsibility seriously for a variety of reasons.

First, public managers are often faced with the task of implementing policies for which both the operational feasibility and the responsible agency's capacity have been insufficiently considered at the formulation stage. They can make both their own and their agency's subsequent implementation task easier and more effective by ensuring that policy formulation is conducted as thoroughly as possible. No less importantly, they may be held responsible if the policy is later found to be poorly designed or ineffective.

Policy formulation also offers opportunities for public managers to represent the interests of individuals and groups without a voice, or with a weak voice, in the policy process. And, at a personal level, policy formation offers public managers an excellent opportunity to hone their skills and to be noticed by their superiors, something that can be of use for their long-term career prospects. Policy formulation thus offers public managers one of their best chances to shape the contours and content of a policy; otherwise, they will largely be involved in implementing and evaluating policies designed by others.

Outside of government there is also a large number of actors who can and do propose and critique policy options. Interest groups, for example, are vital contributors to policy formulation in many countries. Such groups range from professional associations to civil society groups, often closely identified with specific policy issues. However, their role in the policy formulation process is mostly indirect, though no less important, because governments are typically loathe to be seen as being captured by "special interests." Think tanks and universities are also an increasingly vital source of new policy choices. In recent years, public policy education at universities has also grown tremendously, accompanied by a rapid increase in the volume of published research, which provides a good deal of valuable data and evidence about what works, and why (or why not), in many different countries and circumstances. Policy scholars tend, at least avowedly, to be practical in their orientation and strive to offer workable solutions to problems. This practical orientation is even more vital for think tanks. Indeed, their main goal is to offer easily comprehensible analyses of public problems and the solutions to them. The analyses and solutions they offer, which at times will be explicitly partisan, form a rich pool of policy ideas that policy-makers can draw upon in arriving at a range of possible solutions to existing and future policy problems.

As we have seen, these actors, as well as others who are knowledgeable about or have a material interest in the policy in question, come together in policy communities that serve to define, solidify, and support particular policy options in specific sectors and issue areas. The nature of the policy communities makes a great difference to what types of policy options are considered. Some options are open to both new actors and ideas, while others are not, as shown in Table 3.2.

Types of policy options

A useful way to think about the nature of options developed in the policy formulation stage is in terms of the extent to which the proposed alternatives depart from the status quo. Policy alternatives can be categorized into two types based on this criterion: incremental alternatives and fundamental alternatives. *Incremental alternatives*, as the name suggests, are policy alternatives that are only marginally different from the status quo, while *fundamental alternatives* represent a significant departure from the status quo in terms of the ideas they embody, the interests they serve, and the policy instruments they propose.

There is a strong tendency for policy-makers to search for incremental alternatives in policy formulation. This is so for several reasons. First, fundamental overhauls require multiple changes to existing policies and information on the likely impact of such changes is more difficult to obtain. As a result, such alternatives are likely to be set aside on the grounds that they are "unproven" or lack evidence of their efficacy. Second, fundamental alternatives involve a higher risk for many policy-makers because of their generally greater uncertainties and, as a result, the higher degree of risk they entail for budgets, society, political and administrative reputations, and job prospects if something should go terribly wrong. Third, incremental alternatives consume fewer resources because financial, personnel, and organizational arrangements are often already in place and only need to be marginally "tweaked" to implement proposed changes. Finally, the characteristics of large complex organizations—fragmentation, inertia, red tape, and conflicting goals—tend to be strongly biased toward the preservation of the status quo.

This bias toward incremental alternatives has significant implications for policy-making in that it prevents or inhibits the consideration of new solutions to problems even when there is a pressing need for a new course of action. In contemporary areas of concern, such as energy and climate change, for instance, substantial and dramatic changes may be necessary to reverse current trends, requiring policy-makers to look in new directions rather than rework existing practices. But this is very difficult to achieve.

Policy instruments

When policy-makers are exploring policy options, they must consider not only what to do but also how to do it. Thus, while formulating a policy to tackle traffic congestion, for example, policy-makers must simultaneously consider whether to build more roads, improve public transport, restrict automobile usage, or some combination of these, as well as considering the tools by which the policy will actually be implemented. These *policy tools*, also known as *policy instruments* or *governing instruments*, are the actual means or devices that governments use to implement policies.

While the number of generic types of policy tools is limited, each type manifests an almost infinite number of possible variations and combinations, which makes cataloguing all the tools almost impossible. Each generic tool category has its own dynamics and operating

Table 3.1 Examples of policy tools

Private tools	Public tools
Market	Information
Voluntary social organizations	Economic incentives and disincentives
Family	Regulations
	State enterprises
	Direct provision

characteristics, however, and this can lead to some predictable consequences of their use. Even so, many unanticipated effects may become apparent during the course of implementation, possibly arising from unfamiliarity on the part of formulators, decision-makers, and implementors with particular tools, or from the fact that the tool is being used with others in a "policy mix" whose interactive effects are more difficult to predict and control; or from both.

Policy tools may be divided into two main categories, depending on the extent to which they rely on private resources or public authority for their effectiveness (see Table 3.1).

Private instruments involve little or no direct government activity or participation on the basis of the belief that a solution is or will be provided more efficiently and/or effectively by private actors alone. The key forms of private tools are market, family, and voluntary social organizations. When these tools are employed, the desired task is typically performed on a largely voluntary basis by private agents, who may be motivated by financial rewards, emotional satisfaction, religious inspiration, or ideology. Exactly how this may come about and what kinds of goods or services may be provided by what kind of group—family, religious organizations, charities, private firms, and so on—will vary according to the group's motivation, and policy formulators proposing the use of private tools must be aware of the limits and capabilities of the group.

However, it is more common for private instruments to be backed by varying levels of indirect government involvement than to be exercised purely by private actors. Thus, governments not only uphold property rights and enforce contracts, tasks that are essential for markets to work, but they also offer various kinds of subsidies to help shape market behavior and push it in their preferred direction. Similarly, governments provide subsidies and information to help make families and voluntary organizations operate in the manner they desire. Public instruments, on the other hand, are much more direct. They are backed by state sovereignty and/or information that resides within governments and are directed by policy-makers toward certain types of activities, linked to the expected resolution of policy problems. Thus, governments may employ taxes, regulations, or gaol sentences and fines to discourage undesired behavior, construct public enterprises, or provide subsidies to promote desired behavior. In the area of environment protection, for instance, the government may provide subsidies to promote the use of clean technology or they may tax unclean technology. The use of regulations is particularly widespread in controlling economic activities, whereas state enterprises and direct provision are used mostly for providing specific kinds of social goods and services, from public roads to military equipment and defence. The government is also a repository of vast amounts of information that it can use to promote desired behavior (for example, promoting saving water in arid countries) and avoid undesired behavior (for example, discouraging smoking, obesity, unsafe sex, or other health-related issues).

Challenges in policy formulation

Political challenges

The political environment is not always conducive to systematic policy formulation and the consideration of a wide range of policy options. Often senior government officials at the top of the policy pyramid do not know exactly what they want, and will only form ideas in a general way—for example the need for improved access to safe drinking water or the promotion of economic development in a depressed region. At other times they may say things they do not really mean. For example, they may express their commitment to poverty eradication through greater public spending while avoiding the imposition of additional taxes that might decrease their electoral prospects. In such situations, public managers may be at loss to fathom what cues to read in order to formulate appropriate policy options.

Even when political masters know which problems they want to address and express their views transparently, the public may not be supportive of the possible solutions. People dislike traffic congestion in urban areas, for example, but they dislike many solutions even

Table 3.2 Characteristics of policy communities and types of policy change

	Not receptive to new actors	Receptive to new actors
Not receptive to new ideas	Incremental policies (close system)	Policy experimentation (resistant system)
Receptive to new ideas	Program reform (contested system)	Comprehensive policy reform (open system)

more: public transport, because it is inconvenient; more roads, because they could mean more taxes; and the pricing of road use (such as additional charges for licensing, fuel, peak hour road use, or parking), because it is both expensive and inconvenient. To complicate the situation, local residents want to continue to use personal cars while wanting controls against nonresident traffic. This potential public opposition to possible measures to ease traffic congestion is distinct from the opposition of other organs of the government itself. The government agency in charge of small business development, for example, may actually want *more* cars coming into a downtown core in order to enhance patronage of local business by well-heeled suburban consumers. In contrast, an environment agency concerned about the pollution caused by vehicular traffic would be likely to advocate just the opposite.

The nature and composition of the policy community may also pose political challenges for policy formulation. As shown in Table 3.2, some communities are "closed" in that they allow neither new actors nor new ideas to penetrate into the community. In such instances, any option involving major changes will not be seriously entertained. Public managers must be aware of the structure of these networks and the ideas they propound, and be prepared to work with or around them in developing options for senior officials and politicians to consider.

All these contradictory demands and expectations make the task of policy formulation a challenging task indeed. Again, public managers must be acutely aware of the views of, and resources available to, clients, targets, the public, and other members of policy communities, including those in other parts of their government, when proposing solutions to problems. Taking steps to monitor their political environment on a regular basis can go a long way toward helping define and derive a set of policy choices that can address as many conflicting ideas and interests as possible, while avoiding unnecessary conflicts and delays in formulation and other stages of policy-making.

Technical challenges

Despite the priority frequently given to overcoming *political* obstacles, it is often the *technical* barriers that can be most challenging in policy formulation. The difficulties start with understanding the cause of the problem being addressed and the objectives being sought in order to consolidate and scrutinize specific policy options capable of addressing these concerns.

In this regard, when formulating policies, public managers are faced with numerous *substantive* constraints. If there is a lack of a common understanding of the source of a policy problem and no way to determine which of the many possible competing interpretations is correct, for example, managers will find it hard to recognize which objectives to pursue, where to look for alternatives, or what criteria to use to sift or sort policy options. Even when a problem is very narrowly defined— for example, poverty can most simply be defined as a lack of sufficient monetary income—their hands may be tied with respect to the available options. Simply printing more money and distributing it to the poor is inadvisable because the inflation that will result from such an increase in the money supply will offset any gains in income. So one must necessarily address the problem in more complicated ways. Similarly, the problem of global warming cannot be entirely eliminated in the near future because, as yet, there is no known solution to carbon and other greenhouse gas emissions that can be deployed without causing large-scale economic and social disruption in the short term. All of these limitations point to intractability in the technical characteristics of many policy problems.

As a result of these and other substantive constraints, public managers often have to consider a wide range of policy options, many with little or no potential for success, in order to identify measures that might make a net improvement to a situation. While the experience of public managers and their agencies in any one policy sector is an asset in providing information about past efforts to deal with any particular problem, the same experience can also be a barrier to formulating creative options. The current situation may appear normal and in need of only minor improvement, with the result that a proposal for substantial changes might well appear to be an unnecessary aberration.

Institutional challenges

Institutional constraints also exist for effective policy formulation. These have to do with deep-rooted features of the surrounding context that make it difficult to adopt particular policy options or put them into effect. They can take many different forms. Constitutional provisions and the political system form a vital constraint that can limit the range of options available in a given situation. Efforts to control handguns in the US, for example, immediately come up against the constitutional right of citizens to bear arms. The existence of two or more levels of government in federal systems imposes similar constraints because many national policies require intergovernmental agreement, something that can be impossible or very time-consuming to obtain. The nature of political party and electoral systems can also serve to determine a government's "policy horizons," with the result of limiting the kinds of policy options that can be considered feasible for electoral or political reasons. The existence of powerful social groups—physicians, insurers, and pharmaceutical firms in the health care sector, for instance—and their entrenched interests and ideas also casts an indirect but pervasive shadow over the formulation process and can limit the range of alternatives available to governments (such as limiting the possibility of the creation of a national health system in the US and other countries). In a similar vein, specific philosophical or religious ideas can impede potential policy solutions and public managers need to bear these in mind. The manner in which religiously-inspired views on abortion shaped health care reforms in the U.S. Senate in early 2010 is a case in point.

Standard operating procedures in bureaucratic agencies also pose a major institutional barrier to integrated policy formation. While set procedures are vital for upholding the principles of accountability and promoting predictability, they form a barrier to the search for integration and policy innovation. Segmentation of policy authority along sectoral lines, too, poses a hurdle to achieving integration in policy formulation. There is a tendency for each agency to de-emphasize the goals and alternatives that lie outside its immediate domain while promoting its own role. This is a problem because policy problems do not respect sectoral or organizational boundaries and solutions may well, and typically do, transcend such borders.

Strategies for public managers to improve policy formulation

There are numerous ways in which public managers can participate in, and enhance their role in, policy formulation. One very important activity they can undertake is to collect in advance the necessary information on various aspects of emerging and existing problems and develop proposed solutions for use by key policy-makers. They have a special advantage in this role: most policy proposals involve modification of existing policies or programs, with which the public managers are very familiar from their implementation experience. Public managers, especially those with formal training in public policy, are particularly well equipped to ensure that technical issues are given due consideration in policy formulation and to ensure that they are in a position to do so by undertaking early and systematic evidence collection.

Nevertheless, it is often difficult for public managers to play a pro-active role in policy formulation. As mentioned above, the lack of understanding of the causes of the problem being addressed is often an unavoidable difficulty in the formulation stage. Ambitious efforts to prepare for and participate in policy formulation can prove to be fruitless or worse. Depending on the way in which their performance is evaluated, contributions to policy formulation may not benefit and indeed may even hurt public managers' career prospects if they are not equally sensitive to the priorities of powerful actors both within government and also outside it. Moreover, public managers' early involvement in policy formulation carries a danger of being perceived as merely advancing the interests of the agencies they represent. The fragmentation of the policy process across various agencies and layers often only aggravates the problem that proactive agencies may be viewed, correctly or not, as merely guarding their "turf."

Public managers thus need to make special efforts to overcome the difficulties and challenges that hinder their policy formulation efforts. First, they may want to leverage their access to information on existing policies and programs to contribute to the early analysis of reform proposals. The fact that they have implementation experience in the area and that most policy proposals seek only small changes to existing policies works in their favor. Moreover, to bolster their policy capacity, they may need to hire outside experts on the policy issue at hand. Tapping into relevant policy networks can also be useful in making a meaningful contribution to policy formation. All these strategies help to counter the view that their behavior is purely self-interested.

Approaching policy formulation in the following systematic manner thus can help public managers in addressing their policy formulation responsibilities.

Understanding the source of the problem

While studying the root cause of the problem in question is not the purpose of policy formulation, it cannot be avoided. Which options have a fighting chance of being effective depends substantially on what actually caused the problem in the first place. However, often there can be many different interpretations of the causes of problems with no definite means to determine their validity. Some policy problems are so complex—think of poverty, or the banking crises—that there will probably never be full agreement over their true underlying causes, yet policy-makers must do *something* about them. Policy-makers typically respond by selecting a *plausible* interpretation of the source of the problem and then moving on to doing something about it.

In some quarters the need to pinpoint the causes continues to be strongly emphasized. The United Nations Common Country Assessment (CCA), for instance, requires analysis that identifies the immediate, underlying, and root causes of the problems.[1] While this is desirable, it is not possible in many instances, despite the availability of various tools for causality analysis. Thus, while we can identify the different levels of causes of traffic congestion and housing shortages, despite their complexities, it is unlikely that we will ever identify the causes of poverty or school underperformance that will be accepted by all concerned. But, in general, the stronger the evidentiary basis on which policy formulation rests, the greater the likelihood of policy success.

Clarifying policy objectives

Another problem facing public managers is that in order to consider and appraise options, they need to have a sense of the goals they are expected to achieve, and on what time line. While the political executive typically has the primary responsibility for setting overall government objectives, these are often too broad to be applied precisely to specific problem contexts. The task of fleshing-out the objectives falls on those involved in policy formulation. For example, the goal of reducing global warming must be translated into something more specific, such as reducing carbon emissions. But even this is too broad for operational purposes. It falls on public managers to clarify operational objectives so that they can then devise the means to achieve them. To continue the global warming example, this could take the form of specifying the exact targeted percentage decline by a certain year: for example, by 50 percent within 10 years.

With the policy objectives clarified, public managers need to then devise a list of actions that would help achieve the objectives. For example, they would need to consider options such as reducing subsidies or increasing taxes on fossil fuel. What the exact level of tax and/or subsidy would be is a task for decision-making but various options can still be developed at this stage and their potential consequences laid out for decision-makers.

Anticipating changes and building political support

With different and contradictory cues from the political environment, public managers must tread carefully if they are to do their job professionally and effectively. While the lack of clarity or even honesty on the part of the political executive may be a problem, there is little public managers can do to address this. What they can do is to seek as great a degree of transparency as possible, sometimes by clarifying pronouncements on their own and then seeking support and approval from more senior officials for their interpretations.

Once they have arrived at a working interpretation of the sources of the problem and the objectives being sought in addressing it, they need to take additional steps to negotiate the political environment. It is in their professional and personal interest to read the political "winds" while analyzing and reporting possible policy solutions. Thus, while they should consider all plausible solutions fairly, it would be wise to give the most thorough attention to the strengths and weaknesses of the options known to be favored by their political masters.

It might also be sensible to give the same attention to the options proposed by the main opposition party or by groups that may take office or enjoy the more sympathetic ear of government one day in the future. Anticipating and addressing the main lines of concerns of the various powerful social groups is essential. Formal and informal consultation, not only with stakeholders but also with the broader policy network and community, helps effective policy formulation. It not only elicits additional information and insights, but it also helps public managers build support for their analysis and recommendations.

Widespread consultation may, however, also generate additional problems that need to be addressed. It can be time consuming, and can also create opportunities for new lines of opposition to emerge. Public managers have to make their own assessment, based on their experience, as to how much time they can realistically allocate to consultations when faced with deadlines. As a rule of thumb, however, they should err on the side of more consultation rather than less, not least because potential opposition may surface earlier, giving managers more time to respond and adjust policy formulation accordingly.

Formulating policies with implementation in mind

Implementation considerations should be incorporated directly into the design stage of any policy. This is particularly important where policies are long term in their approach. There are several ways to do this.

Starting relatively small while building support for more integrated policies will be warranted when the key issues are contested or are surrounded by grave uncertainties. There are a range of unknowns at the outset of any complex initiative for policy change, not least regarding the incentives faced by, and inclinations of, the different actors who must work together. Thus, conceiving smaller-scale initiatives as "policy experiments" can help facilitate adaptive implementation—the ability to learn what works, and how to fix what *isn't* working, in the process of implementation itself. The design of projects as adaptive policy experiments implies the existence of strong information systems, a point reinforced in later chapters.

Another key to the proper design of policies from an implementation perspective is to systematically review their logical construction *prior* to the implementation stage itself. The basic intention is to test the degree to which policies are logically constructed so that invested inputs stand a realistic chance of being processed into project outputs, which themselves contribute reliably to the required outcomes. "Forward mapping" and "backward mapping" are two related tools that may assist in the attempt to ensure policies are logically and soundly designed to achieve their stated aims, and that all the elements required for implementation are "assembled" and in place (see Box 3.1).

Looking beyond incremental changes

With causes determined and objectives set, no matter how imprecisely, public managers can move to developing options. The options may emerge from a variety of sources, including: (i) policy modelling, (ii) policy transfer, and (iii) policy innovation.

One way to generate options is to *model the problem* by identifying probable causes. For example, the problem of deforestation can be

Box 3.1 Forward and backward mapping

In forward mapping, otherwise known as scenario analysis, the analyst writes out for him- or herself how implementation is implicitly *supposed* to take place (if it is to be successful), including all the relevant actors, their roles, and the sequence and orchestration of their actions. The analyst then uses this narrative as the basis for two fundamental critiques:

- Critique 1: Is each of the actors actually likely to be sufficiently incentivized and capable of acting in the manner prescribed?
- Critique 2: Might any *other* actor affected by the policy get involved and potentially interfere with or deflect policy intentions during implementation, and if so, can they actually be stopped from doing so?

Based on the answers to these questions, the analyst then rewrites the scenario to make it more realistic, including preventive and other measures to enhance the likelihood of success.

Backward mapping—sometimes labelled "bottom-up policy design"—involves first specifying the actual behaviors that need to take place in order that policy outcomes will be achieved. For instance, in order to achieve the policy goal of cleaning up city canals, one might specify the behavioral change that "city inhabitants no longer throw their garbage into the canal." Having identified the specific behaviors to be changed, the analyst *then* designs policies from different logical options that can help achieve this objective, paying special attention to how the intervention can practically motivate the required changes in behavior.

These analytical tools are in some ways quite commonsensical and straightforward. But they may prove surprisingly useful in anticipating policy implementation problems, and in brainstorming alternative policy options to increase the likelihood of success in implementation.

Source: D. Weimer and A. Vining (1992) *Policy Analysis: Concepts and Practice*, Englewood Cliffs, NJ: Prentice Hall, pp. 402–406.

modelled by looking at several plausible causes that can be influenced by policy intervention. These causes can be categorized into five groups:

1. poor governance;
2. insufficient attention to the local community;
3. poor consultation processes;
4. limited or conflicting information; and
5. problems with existing laws and regulations.

Within each of the probable causes lies a possible solution. Thus, if poor governance is believed to be the key problem, then the answer possibly lies in strengthening governance in the forestry sector. However, modelling of problems does not necessarily lead to the generation of specific policy options. Rather, it helps to identify the "intervening variables" that the policy options might be designed to affect. It is risky to leap from an "intervening variable" to a single policy proposal, because the policy proposed may not achieve the required change for the variable, or it could even cause a whole new set of problems to emerge.

Policy options can also be generated by learning from policies used elsewhere, through *policy transfer*. This process is sometimes also referred to as "borrowing" and "tinkering." For example, the use of economic incentives in environmental protection that originated in the West has been transferred to many developing countries in dealing with their environmental challenges. Privatization and deregulation of telecommunications in the UK and civil aviation in the US in the early 1980s were similarly widely emulated in other countries in subsequent years. The challenges for sustainable development are remarkably similar in many countries, for example, and there are increased opportunities to "learn" from experiences of policy interventions elsewhere. A technique as simple as searching the Internet is currently one of the most widely used practices among policy-makers seeking to ascertain what is being done about any given problem in other jurisdictions. Other more formal mechanisms also exist for this purpose—for example, regional associations such as the OECD, ASEAN, and APEC or international ones such as the IMF and the World Bank.

The "tinkering" process is essential for the success of policies generated through policy transfer because policy environments differ substantially across jurisdictions and across countries. The "tinkering" process typically involves four steps:

1. to decompose an alternative into its essential components;
2. to identify different designs for the components;
3. to reassemble the designs into alternatives; and
4. to select those combinations that look most promising.

Knowledge of foreign and other practices, however, may not always be readily available for public managers to access and innovate upon. Again, early work and continual environmental scans on the part of prescient managers may prove invaluable in this regard.

Policy innovation is another vital source for policy choices. Innovation may consist of developing something entirely new or useful or, as is more common, employing existing practices or arrangements in new ways for new uses. Innovative use of policy tools is particularly fruitful for those looking for new ideas. One such instance is Singapore's use of the auction of ownership rights to curb the purchase of cars, a practice borrowed from the environment sector where pollution rights are auctioned to firms in polluting industries. Another example is the imposition of fossil fuel taxes coupled with the removal of employment related taxes; these would simultaneously address the problems of carbon emissions and unemployment without affecting the government's overall finances. Partnership with the private sector may also improve services without raising costs. International trade in carbon credits is an interesting use of private incentives to serve environmental causes. Again, however, public managers require experience and expert researchers in order to develop feasible innovations.

Leveraging on policy networks

Public managers may personally or collectively only be familiar with a limited range of possible options and the tools required for putting them into effect. This makes it difficult for them to recommend new or innovative options and tools. Better research and hiring of experienced and well-trained analysts is essential for overcoming this problem. Commissioning outside consultants to recommend policy options is another alternative they may employ.

Consultation with other members of the policy community, however, is another inexpensive way to overcome technical challenges. Such consultations allow public managers to understand the depth and breadth of the problem as well as the urgency with which it needs to be addressed. The various relevant interest groups, policy-makers, and researchers often have an extensive knowledge of policy problems and potential solutions, which can offer a valuable source of information and insight. Consultations can also generate information on the lines and depth of opposition to, and support for, particular policy options being considered, enabling public managers to accommodate and respond to the reservations expressed.

Consolidating and screening options

Considering as many viable solutions as possible is vital. But so is keeping the list of options being considered relatively small. There are often many possible alternative policies for tackling a given policy problem, but a lack of time, information, and money typically make it impossible to systematically examine all of them. It is therefore important to narrow down the list of policy options through consolidation and screening. The task of consolidating the numerous policy options that typically emerge during the early phases of policy formulation consists of several related activities:

1. Policy options should be categorized based on whether or not they are mutually exclusive. When they are found to be not exclusive, they should either be clarified to make them distinct or excluded from the list.
2. A distinction should be made between a basic alternative and its variants. The distinction is especially helpful when there are a lot of possible solutions and there is a need to reduce the complexity of choice. Making such distinctions can help a manager break the analysis into successive steps, facilitating the decision-making stage later on.
3. The third task is to make policy options comparable, based on the scales of their impacts or costs. It is difficult to compare alternatives properly when such scales are dramatically different.

The *feasibility* of policy choices should be used as an explicit criterion to systematically screen various alternatives. It makes little sense to devote time and resources to policy choices that are clearly infeasible.

A feasible policy choice must be politically acceptable or at least not patently unacceptable. A policy option may be infeasible because, for example, it cannot be expected to gain the approval necessary to legitimize it, or because the political support needed for policy implementation is not in place. Arnold Meltsner has developed a useful checklist to assess the political acceptability of policy different alternatives. *Who* are the relevant actors? *What* are their motivations and beliefs? *What* are their political resources? *In which* political arenas will the relevant decisions be made?

While it is important to screen out infeasible policy choices in the short term, one should not take a static view of feasibility. Circumstances change. What may have been infeasible in the past may be feasible today or in the future. Many of the environmental protection measures adopted recently were not thinkable even a decade ago before concerns with phenomena such as global warming arose on the policy agenda.

Additionally, new policy choices may emerge during the screening process. For example, someone may realize that certain features of an alternative increase the cost disproportionately to its contribution to effectiveness, leading to a search for alternatives that are equally effective but less costly. Similarly, as effectiveness is explored, new features may be found to increase effectiveness with little added cost.

Establishing and participating in interagency committees or task forces

Interagency committees or task forces can also help with effective policy formulation, especially when a problem may be the responsibility of one agency but has implications for many others with enough power to stall the proposal during decision-making or implementation. Setting up interministerial committees or task forces to deal with foreign direct investments, for example, helps to formulate policies that can potentially incorporate the interests and objectives of different government agencies. Policy-makers can create processes for representing groups or resolving disputes—by appointing a committee, calling in a mediator, or seeking to change the power balance by creating an independent commission or changing the powers and resources enjoyed by certain key players.

Conclusion

Policy formulation is a key stage of policy-making and one in which astute public managers may find their greatest opportunity to affect decision-making and policy implementation. It is a complex stage involving a range of actors with different ideas about and different interests in the promotion of specific solutions to policy problems. Public managers need to ensure that they have the appropriate levels of analytical, administrative, and political knowledge and capacity to adequately carry out the many tasks involved in policy design and appraisal.

Once this is done, however, they can be more confident that the proposals that go on to decision-makers for adjudication and decision will be capable of "doing the job" and will not make a situation worse. It is to this decision-making activity that we now turn in the following chapter.

Note

1   See United Nations (2007) *Common Country Assessment and United Nations Development Assistance Framework*. Available online at www.undg.org/ docs/6860/2007%20CCA%20and%20UNDAF%20Guidelines%20FINAL.doc.

Further reading

Bardach, Eugene (2000) *A Practical Guide For Policy Analysis: The Eightfold Path To More Effective Problem Solving*. New York: Chatham House Publishers.

Bryson, J. M., G. L. Cunningham, and K. J. Lakkemoe (2002) "What to Do When Stakeholders Matter: The Case of Problem Formulation for the African American Men Project of Hennepin County, Minnesota" *Public Administration Review* 62(5): 568–84.

deLeon, P. (1992) "Policy Formulation: Where Ignorant Armies Clash by Night" *Policy Studies Review* 11(3/4): 389–405.

Freed, G. L., M. C. Andreae, A. E. Cowan, and S. L. Katz (2002) "The Process of Public Policy Formulation: The Case of Thimerosal in Vaccines" *Pediatrics* 109(6): 1153–59.

Gonsalves J., T. Becker, A. Braun, D. Campilan, H. De Chavez, E. Fajber, M. Kapiriri, J. Rivaca-Caminade, and R. Vernooy (Eds.) (2005) P*articipatory Research and Development for Sustainable Agriculture and Natural Resource Management: A Sourcebook*. International Potato Center—Users' Perspectives with Agricultural Research and Development, Laguna, Philippines and International Development Research Centre, Ottawa, ON, Canada, Volume 3.

Howlett, M., M. Ramesh, and A. Perl. (2009) *Studying Public Policy: Policy Cycles and Policy Subsystems*. Oxford: Oxford University Press.

James, Thomas E. and Paul D. Jorgensen (2009) "Policy Knowledge, Policy Formulation, and Change: Revisiting a Foundational Question" *Policy Studies Journal* 37(1): 141–62.

Lester, James P. and Joseph Stewart (2000) *Public Policy: An Evolutionary Approach*. Belmont, CA: Wadsworth.

MacRae, D. and D. Whittington (1997) *Expert Advice for Policy Choice: Analysis and Discourse*. Washington, DC: Georgetown University Press.

Meltsner, Arnold J. (1972) "Political Feasibility and Policy Analysis" *Public Administration Review* 32(6): 859–67.

Putt, A. and J. Springer (1989) *Policy Research: Concepts, Methods, and Applications*, Upper Saddle River, NJ: Prentice Hall.

Rajagopalan, Nandini and Abdul M. A. Rasheed (1995) "Incremental Models of Policy Formulation and Non-Incremental Changes: Critical Review and Synthesis" *British Journal of Management* 6: 289–302.

Thomas, H. G. (2001) "Towards a New Higher Education Law in Lithuania: Reflections on the Process of Policy Formulation" *Higher Education Policy* 14(3): 213–23.

Weimer, D. and A. Vining (1992) *Policy Analysis: Concepts and Practice*, Upper Saddle River, NJ: Prentice Hall.

4 Decision-making

Decision-making is the policy function in which a decision is made to take a course of action (or non-action) to deal with a policy problem. It is an extremely important stage of the policy process, often involving a relatively small group of high-level officials authorized to bind the government to a specific course of action, taking into account a range of political and technical considerations and analyses. However, it is a misconception to think that public managers are not involved in decision-making. Depending on the organization(s) they serve, public managers may make policy decisions by themselves, may provide policy recommendations for higher-level policy-makers, and may provide advice and information on different policy options under consideration by senior decision-makers. This chapter highlights the opportunities and potential for public managers to be involved in decision-making as well as the strategies and analytical tools they can employ to reduce the incoherencies and inconsistencies, widespread in the policy process, that originate at this stage of policy-making.

The basics of decision-making

What is decision-making?

Decision-making is the stage of policy-making involving the selection of a course of action from a range of policy options, *including* that of maintaining the status quo. It is not synonymous with the entire policy-making process, although it is sometimes discussed as if this were so. Decision-making is distinguishable from agenda setting and policy formulation, for example, in both the key features of the tasks and also the narrower range of key players involved. It is also broader in scope than policy adoption as the latter only focusses on the final step in decision-making for certain policies and tends to ignore the processes leading up the adoption of a new or revised policy.

The decision-making process varies across decision-makers and the contexts in which they operate. For example, different countries have different constitutional and organizational arrangements and operating procedures, all of which have significant impacts on the decision-making processes they follow. In addition, decision-making processes are also influenced by the nature of the decision-makers themselves. They will vary in background, knowledge, and value systems, and this in turn will affect how they approach their tasks and the factors they consider in decision-making. As a result of these contextual factors, decision-makers in different settings respond differently when dealing with the same or similar problems. However, they also share some common motivations and patterns of policy-making behavior, which provide structure and continuity, and an element of predictability, to their choices and selections.

Main actors in decision-making

It is a common perception among public managers that decision-making is, more or less, the exclusive business of senior administrators and/or elected officials, and is therefore dominated by political rather than administrative or technical considerations. Decision-making is indeed highly political because policy decisions often create "winners" or "losers," whose real and anticipated reactions to the different policy options play an essential role in shaping policy decisions. However, it is a misconception among many public managers that policy decisions are driven solely by political considerations. Other considerations—for example, the potential effectiveness of policies in achieving the intended policy goals and their impacts on society in the long term—are also important and demand technical expertise and professional analysis. Decision-making is thus often more technical, and less political, than assumed.

And, while it is true that elite members of governments are the main players in formal decision-making, public policies may take many forms, and public managers can be involved in decision-making in various capacities. First of all, public policy decisions can be acts, laws, regulatory guidance, and/or procedural measures, many of which may be decided at different levels of government agencies so that the final elite "decision" is merely to approve a kind of patchwork of previous, subordinate choices made by public managers in other locations. This is especially the case where the policy issues or solutions are highly technical. The top-level approval in such cases is often merely a procedural requirement rather than substantive in nature. Second, even for the policies for which substantial input from top executives and legislative bodies is sought, the policy options reaching these decision-makers typically reflect the preferences and alternatives developed by public managers at various levels within the government. Third, even when they do not propose specific alternatives, public managers are often asked by high-level policy-makers to prepare appraisals or evaluations of their preferred policy options, or to provide technical information and professional advice on various aspects of those options, such as effectiveness and administrative feasibility, again allowing public managers to have a significant impact on any final decisions that flow from these deliberations and choices.

There are also other actors involved in decision-making, such as professional analysts, issue-specific experts, consultants, and lobbyists, although their participation can best be categorized as indirect since their influence is felt indirectly through their affiliations or associations with decision-makers rather than directly upon the adoption of a policy choice. For example, professional analysts in the Congressional Budget Office (CBO) in the US are regularly involved in providing policy analysis on key policy decisions facing legislators. In some, relatively rare, instances the public can also be involved in decision-making when public referenda are used. In 1959, for example, a Swiss national referendum rejected women's rights to vote. It was not until 26 years later that another referendum gave voting rights to women.

Ultimately, the organizational aspects of policy and administration are critical in decision-making, because, in the end, policies are carried out or supervised by specific government agencies. The capacities of these agencies in policy implementation and adaptation play an essential role in shaping policy decisions through their impact on considerations of the feasibility of policy choices.

This tripod of political, technical, and organizational considerations is a distinct feature of public policy decision-making, compared to decision-making in the private sector, which is usually more focussed on criteria such as profit-making. The public policy decision-makers' ability to integrate these three aspects in their choices often determines the overall effectiveness of the policies they adopt in dealing with government public concerns and so it is important that public managers should ensure that this integration happens.

Decision-making models

Policy scientists use a variety of models to capture the dynamics of public policy decision-making. They categorize decision-making into three main models depending on the extent to which information is known about expected policy outcomes.

The "rational" decision model

The first model is a "rational" decision model, which is built on the assumption that the consequences of each alternative policy option can be known in advance. According to this model, decision-makers should choose the option that maximizes the attainment of their individual goals, values, and objectives. The model is "rational" in the sense that, at least in theory, it can lead to the most efficient way of achieving policy goals. Although the rational decision model is appealing in normative terms, the applicability of the model is hampered by the need for a large amount of accurate information on policy impacts and consequences, which may be impractical or impossible to obtain in the usually short time frame in which decision-makers have to act. It also assumes a uniformity of purpose among decision-makers, which may well be lacking. When the consequences of various options are not known with certainty, the time to gather more information and make better comparisons is not usually available, and when decisions are made by a number of decision-makers, the outcomes of a "rational" process are likely to be less good and less efficient than expected or hoped.

The limitations of the rational decision model have led to the development of alternative decision frameworks intended to model outcomes when circumstances are less than ideal.

The "incremental" decision model

The first alternative is the "incremental" decision model, which analyzes public decision-making as a time- and information-constrained process characterized by conflict, bargaining, and compromise among self-interested decision-makers. Rather than adopt "maximizing" alternatives, in this model it is expected that decisions arrived at through bargaining will be the result of the "successive limited comparisons" decision-makers make of new proposals against the results of earlier decisions, resulting typically in only "marginal" or "incremental" changes from the status quo. In this model, the decisions eventually made represent more what is politically feasible in the sense of satisfying the interests of various participants rather than what might be technically desirable in a more certain policy climate. According to Lindblom,[1] the reasons why policy decisions typically do not stray far away from the status quo are:

1. since the status quo already represents an interest-based compromise, it is politically more feasible to continue the existing pattern of distribution of goods and services than to alter the system dramatically through a redistribution typically required of any radically new proposals; and
2. the standard operating procedures and administrative practices of bureaucracies charged with implementing existing policies also tend to favor minor modifications of existing practices instead of their major overhaul.

The "garbage can" decision model

The second alternative to rational decision models is the so-called "garbage can" model, which applies when there is a very large number of decision-makers and a great deal of uncertainty about both the causes of problems and their solutions. It is argued that, in such situations, policy outcomes will lack even the modest semblance of rationality found in incrementalism and will instead reflect the temporary desires of those actually able to dominate, however transitorily, the decision-making process. In this model, the ideas of maximization, found in the rational model, or of optimization, found in the incremental model, are largely abandoned. Instead it is argued that a *satisficing* principle is likely to emerge, in which decision-making involves simply satisfying whatever standards or goals have been set by a group of policy-makers at the time of the decision. According to this model, the search for a policy response to a policy problem will end when a policy option at hand is perceived to be able to produce "acceptable" results as defined by the standards set by influential decision-makers, and the range of policy choices with potentially better results is never fully explored. Decision-makers thus would look beyond the relatively small range of policy options at hand only if these options fail to produce a satisfactory or *satisficing* outcome.

Challenges in decision-making

While these frameworks vary dramatically in terms of the nature of the circumstances in which they are expected to apply, and in terms of the kinds of choices that typically emerge from them, underlying all three models is the idea that public policy decision-making consists of:

1. the presence of one or more policy proposals to be decided upon based on their relationship to the possible resolution of the policy problem defined at earlier stages of the policy process;

2. the presence of a set of decision criteria, however loosely articulated in practice, based on decision-makers' policy goals and other considerations;
3. some efforts at comparison and ranking of policy proposals based on the set of decision criteria established; and
4. determination of a policy option to be implemented in subsequent phases of the policy process.

The above outline of the decision-making process, however, allows a great deal of variation in how decisions are made in practice in many different circumstances and many different countries and sectors. In the absence of a logical and orderly process of searching for means to achieve policy goals and developing criteria for alternative assessment, decisions are often made in an ad hoc and haphazard manner, even when adequate information and time are available and the decision-making context is appropriate to allow a closer approximation to the rational model. Thus, for example:

1. Policy decisions, even on technical issues, are often dominated by immediate imperatives and made on an ad hoc basis without careful consideration of their broader and longer-term implications. During the 1997–98 Asian financial crisis, for example, a series of ad hoc decisions by the Suharto government in Indonesia contributed to the worsening of the economy and eventually led to its own collapse. Poor policy planning in noncrisis situations can also lead to similarly poor results, as when, for example, decision-makers run up against electoral or parliamentary timetables and are forced to curtail their policy deliberations and adopt ill-considered or "quick" decisions.
2. Policy decisions can be hijacked by ideological obsessions or even by the fantasies of political leaders. For example, the Great Leap Forward in China in the 1950s, which was responsible for millions of deaths from famine and other causes, was largely motivated by the unrealistic aspirations of Mao Zedong, China's leader at the time. More recently, the ideological conviction on the part of policy-makers in several developing countries that the adoption of market principles could improve policy outcomes and efficiency in many sectors also led to an ill-considered rush to privatize and deregulate many industries and social services, moves that were subsequently followed by renationalization and reregulation of many of these activities.

3. Poor decisions can also arise when policy decisions are controlled and manipulated by a small number of political executives and/or a small number of policy advisers closely associated with decision-making. This happens when a group's personal and institutional biases have a detrimental impact on the quality of their decisions and, subsequently, on policy outcomes. This is commonly the case with many military, police, and authoritarian regimes, as in the case of Mao Zedong in China cited above, but can also happen in more pluralistic states. For example, the domination of decision-making processes by the small groups of national security advisers surrounding U.S. President George W. Bush and UK Prime Minister Tony Blair led to ill-informed decisons to invade Iraq in 2003, despite the existence of analytical capacities rivalling those of any government in the world.

4. Poor outcomes also can result from policy decisions made without careful attention to their practicality, leading to large gaps between policy design and implementation. In the Philippines, for example, a decision to decentralize key social services, such as health and education, from central to local government was made without due attention being paid to the lack of planning capacity at the local level in that particular country. Bureaucrats with the necessary experience and skills in planning are often reluctant to be reallocated from capital cities, and without them decision-making in the regions can flounder.

5. A similar situation can result when policy decisions made by one agency are inconsistent and even in conflict with policies implemented by other agencies. This lack of "horizontality," for example, is apparent in many countries in areas such as sustainable development and environmental protection, which require a great deal of intra- and intergovernmental coordination—something that is often lacking. This can result in situations, for example, where employment incentives are offered to industries to locate in regions that are environmentally sensitive, and are undergoing enhanced protection from parks and wilderness agencies.

6. And, of course, in many democratic countries, as well as non-democratic ones, policy decisions can sometimes be determined largely by purely political considerations, such as elections and the balancing of interest groups, while policy proposals with true potential in achieving policy goals can be overlooked by decision-makers.

In addition to the above shortcomings, which are primarily structural and political in nature, decision-makers aspiring to improve decision-making processes are also confronted with the following set of challenges, which are technical and organizational in nature:

1. *Short time horizon.* As we have seen, the time horizon facing decision-makers is often too short to adequately assess the various effects of policy proposals, especially those that deviate significantly from current policies and practices. As a result, long-term benefits and costs may be hard to identify and anyway may be given much less weight than the short-term and more immediately obvious ones, or may be ignored altogether.
2. *Lack of reliable information.* Information needed for adequately assessing different policy options is often unavailable or available only at a very high cost. In many developing countries, low priority is given to the collection of data and information, and, as a result, government agencies often do not have reliable information critical to decision-making on hand when they need it.
3. *Lack of expertise in policy analysis.* The analysis of policy proposals can be highly complex, but very few government officials possess the necessary training and experience to carry out proper analysis. The situation is further compounded in many developing countries where remuneration for civil servants is relatively low compared to the private sector, and thus government agencies often lose out to the private sector in competition to recruit or retain professional analysts with adequate training and skills.
4. *Performance measurement inside the bureaucracy.* The performance of government agencies responsible for certain policy areas is often measured against their mandated goals, which traditionally are defined in a single dimension, such as efficiency. Therefore, there is a strong tendency to favor a single dimension in decision-making rather than attributes with multiple dimensions, such as sustainability, equity, or justice.

Strategies and analytical tools for public managers in decision-making

Integrating and mandating political, technical, and organizational considerations

A common shortcoming in decision-making in reality is that important considerations beyond immediate policy goals are often neglected. It is important that the right criteria are chosen for decision-making, however, because the use of different decision criteria can lead to different judgments with regard to the relative merits of policy choices. Decision criteria may differ from policy objectives, which are often expressed in a single dimension and in vague terms such as "cutting pollution by 50 percent" or "increasing access to safe drinking water for the poor." More explicit and specific decision criteria can help to clarify these objectives by proposing standards that are measurable and, most importantly, help policy-makers to focus attention on the potential constraints and interlinkages among policy objectives across different policy sectors. This latter feature of decision criteria is critical for the pursuit of sustainable development, for example, which requires the joint consideration of multiple objectives. Missing a critical criterion may lead to poor decisions—as the consequences that would have been measured by the missing criterion could potentially have shifted the calculation of costs of and benefits of decisions made by decision-makers and administrators.

Improvements in this area can be achieved through better determination of decision criteria. Policy decisions are made to advance objectives that are of value to the society (or at least certain segments in the society). Decision criteria thus guide decision-making by providing standards against which policy consequences can be judged as being important or valuable. In addition, decision criteria are used to measure the practicality of various options. The use of the same criteria across different policy options ensures that the alternatives can be compared systematically. Criteria commonly used in assessing the consequences of policy options include: efficiency, effectiveness, equity, feasibility, and political acceptability as well as, ever more frequently, sustainability.

In general, compared to economic outcomes, it takes a long time for environmental and social impacts to manifest themselves, and thus often less attention is paid to these aspects of a decision. For example, merely reporting pollution levels may not capture the decision-makers' and the public's imaginations and so they may not appreciate the severity of an environmental problem, unless the levels are related to how they could affect daily life. Therefore, criteria need to be selected strategically so that they represent concerns of importance to decision-makers and the public. For example, using health threats as criteria may be more effective in communicating the importance of environmental impacts than presenting environmental impacts in terms of pollution levels.

Mandating and requiring decision-makers to jointly consider the key objectives of a multi-criteria policy can help balance the inclinations of governmental agencies to emphasize only those goals or objectives with which they are most closely associated, since imposing mandatory requirements can often ensure that multiple key objectives are considered in all policy decisions. Because of the difficulties and resource implications of such analyses, organizations will have little incentive to develop such resources unless they are mandated, and imposing such requirements helps strengthen public managers' arguments for the need for capacity-building in their agency in order to properly assess impacts (which their organizations may not be accustomed to evaluate).

Imposing such requirements can also help organizations to develop policy options and evidence that highlight synergies among seemingly conflicting objectives and expand the horizons of organizations in search of innovative solutions.

Basing decisions on systematic analysis

Establishing a baseline is the first critical step toward more systematic analysis. A "baseline," also referred to as a "business as usual" scenario, describes what would happen if there were no change in government decisions and existing trends continued. It provides a necessary knowledge base for assessments of the effects of proposed and actual policy interventions. Note that this baseline is different from the status quo because there can be changes from the status quo due to naturally occurring changes and effects of other policies in existence. The time span for a baseline assessment should be the same as the time horizon used to assess policy options.

Because a baseline is different from the status quo and requires extrapolation of current trends and calculation of their effects, collecting the information necessary for establishing a policy baseline is technically challenging and time-consuming. The following information is required to establish such a baseline:

- current conditions (or status quo);
- current and expected trends;
- effects of policies already being implemented; and
- effects of other foreseeable policies or programs.

The baseline provides an essential reference point against which various policy options can be compared. Without the baseline, the option of "let present trends continue" is typically dropped out of consideration, leaving the door open for policy interventions that might aggravate policy problems rather than improve them. Sometimes poorly designed policies are worse than no policy at all.

Assessing economic, social, and environmental impacts of policy options

The second critical step, once criteria have been chosen and a baseline established, is to project the likely outcomes of different policy options against each individual criterion. Such a task is the most challenging, and technical, part of the decision-making process, since it involves projecting into the future, which is inherently uncertain (despite the availability of various tools and techniques to try to take this uncertainty into account). While various techniques and tools can be used to address the challenges imposed by uncertainty in assessment, they cannot remove it entirely.

Assessment aims at providing the following information to public managers and policy-makers:

- solid empirical information—data- or evidence-derived—about the likely direction of economic, social, and environmental changes resulting from the policy options under consideration;
- solid evidence about the nature and order of magnitude of changes; and
- solid evidence about the duration and reversibility of changes.

Decision-making is typically confronted with various uncertainties because information to support accurate predictions of the outcome of policy choices is often inadequate. But there are different types of uncertainty depending on whether they are related to knowledge of the policy problem and its trends, or to the impact of policy solutions, or to uncertainties regarding the policy process itself and its outcomes. Some can be handled with statistical methods, while others can be reduced through further research. However, some uncertainties are inherent and cannot be reduced. For example, predictions with regard to global warming are inherently uncertain and cast a constant shadow over policy debate on climate change.

The projection of outcomes nevertheless remains of utmost importance in the policy decision-making process. Policy-makers should be cautious about, and try to avoid or overcome, the following three biases often found in assessments:

- *A bias toward criteria for which quantitative measures are available.* Some impacts might not be quantified because of a gap in data, despite their vital importance. Qualitative measures of these impacts should be developed by relying on judgment informed by experience and knowledge.

- *A bias toward positive impacts.* Both positive impacts and negative impacts are critical in assessing policy options, and overlooking negative impacts can easily lead to poor decisions.
- *A bias toward the study of impacts of a particular dimension,* closely associated with the identity of the organizations conducting the assessment.

Comparing policy options

The third step is to compare policy options based on their predicted effects. Establishing a baseline and assessing projected impacts can generate an immense amount of information and, therefore, there is a need to systematize the collection and display of that information. The assessment of various options provides opportunities for policy innovation, as information revealed through a comparison of different options can aid policy design by prompting the reformulation of certain options and the identification of mitigation strategies for others. Various components in different options can be reconfigured into new combinations that might then lead to win-win options, and mitigation strategies can be developed to reduce particular negative impacts for options that are preferable along other dimensions. Too much attention is often devoted to the trade-offs between different objectives, while innovative opportunities for synergy are overlooked. Identification of opportunities and synergies is a hallmark of integrated decision-making.

In most cases, implicit or explicit trade-offs are still required in the decision-making process. Before value judgments are made on how trade-offs would be settled, it is critical to identify them, and the use of decision matrices can facilitate the process. (See Box 4.1.)

It must be recalled, however, that policy analysis, regardless of how comprehensive it appears, is but one input for decision-makers in their decision-making, and a final decision can be made not to adopt a policy option even though it might be ranked best in all dimensions. Political imperatives, narrowly defined agency interests, and decision-makers' self-interests are important considerations for decision-makers in making their final decisions and, as we have seen, the final decision is often the outcome of the strategic interaction and compromise among multiple decision-makers.

The highly political nature of some decisions, however, does not imply that the value of sound analysis should be discounted. The assessment can effectively set a boundary within which trade-offs can be made between political imperatives and technical merits. For example, it is much easier to reject the worst policy choice when its negative

Box 4.1 Decision matrix

A convenient way to systematically organize information required for effective decision-making is to display it in the form of a decision matrix, which typically will display policy choices across the columns and decision criteria down the rows. Any cell in the decision matrix contains the projected outcome of the alternative assessed by reference to the column criterion. For example, Cell A1 contains information on the outcome of Alternative A as assessed by reference to Criterion 1.

To aid the decision-making process, each alternative in the matrix should be linked to each criterion systematically. To protect against or counter the biases of the analyst, all cells should be considered, which promotes recognition and discussion of oversights and biases.

Criteria	Alternative A	Alternative B	Alternative C	Alternative . . .
Criterion 1	A1	B1	C1	. . .
Criterion 2	A2	B2	C2	. . .
Criterion 3	A3	B3	C3	. . .
Criterion . . .				. . .

Source: D. MacRae and D. Whittington (1997) *Expert Advice for Policy Choice: Analysis and Discourse*. Washington, DC: Georgetown University Press.

impacts are conclusively indicated by the analysis, and by the same token, it creates a tremendous hurdle for policy-makers to ignore a win-win solution when it has been clearly identified.

Of course, things can get decidedly more complicated for decision-making when trade-offs between different dimensions of a problem are necessary. However, sound analysis remains of great value in ensuring a sound decision, not least because it forces the decision-makers to openly share their values with other actors. In a democratic context the other actors might often include stakeholders or the general public, who both can benefit from the provision of good information about various policy options. Such information can help enable them to participate at a higher level and to have a greater impact in the decision-making process.

Strengthen policy analysis capacity

The importance of the careful analysis of policy options doesn't imply that all public managers themselves ought to be experts in all of the techniques and applications of policy analysis. Public managers, however, can play an instrumental role in fostering the development of policy analysis capacity both within and outside government. They can take advantage of the fast development of public policy programs across many countries by recruiting professional analysts with proper training in policy analysis, and they can also send their staff to short training courses to strengthen their analytical capacity. It is important to provide institutional support for professional analysts, such as the creation and support of dedicated department units, or "policy shops," focussing on policy analysis and planning, as well as ensuring there are adequate resources to them to be able to carry out their work, thus making policy analysis an attractive career development path for new recruits.

Public managers should also contribute to the development of policy analytical capacity outside government by easing restrictions on access to information. Competition is a powerful tool that can drive innovation and quality improvement and can be harnessed to improved decision-making. Promoting competition in internal and external policy assessments can often save costs, improves both the data and the techniques available to decision-makers, and can help to bridge knowledge gaps that exist in the understanding of key policy issues. It may also help to reduce the risk of having assessments hijacked by narrowly defined organizational and personal interests. The role of independent researchers and consultants in such assessments should be strengthened to promote competition with internal government analysts. The assessments conducted by these organizations and individuals are less likely to be constrained by the sorts of political and institutional constraints facing government agencies and may thus offer more balanced and objective assessment to aid decision-making. But, to be effective, such assessments require that governments be more transparent and share information with other governmental and nongovernmental agencies.

Improving intra-agency and interagency linkage in decision-making

As mentioned above, many contemporary policy problems are multi-dimensional in nature and these dimensions easily cross jurisdictional and other boundaries established in previous eras. This is especially true of vertically-"siloed" government agencies, which are structured

64   *Decision-making*

to pursue specific notions of the origins and solutions of policy problems. Public managers can promote "horizontality," that is, the creation of international, intergovernmental, or interagency bodies that can help to remove policy consideration from the one-dimensional or limited nature of analysis performed in agency silos. Enhanced conversations, consultations, and cooperation with other members of the policy community within and outside the government can be expected to lead to more soundly judged decisions.

Conclusion

Policy decisions cap the process of policy-making, which started with agenda setting and was then sifted through formulation. The decision-making stage of the policy process is more political than the preceding processes, in that it is handled by more senior appointed and elected officials, but it is also more technical. In addition to astute political judgment, the success of decision-making depends on evidence and sound analysis, something that public managers are best placed to offer. They need to rise to this challenge if public policies are not to falter at the implementation stage, the subject of the following chapter.

Note

1   Lindblom, C. E. (1959) "The Science of Muddling Through" *Public Administration Review* 19(2): 79–88.

Further reading

Bardach, Eugene (2000) *A Practical Guide for Policy Analysis: The Eightfold Path to more Effective Problem Solving*. New York: Chatham House Publishers.
Braybrooke, D. and C. Lindblom (1963) *A Strategy of Decision: Policy Evaluation as a Social Process*. New York: Free Press of Glencoe.
Cohen, M., J. March, and J. Olsen (1972) "A Garbage Can Model of Organizational Choice" *Administrative Science Quarterly* 17(1): 1–25.
Hood, C. (1999) "The Garbage Can Model of Organization: Describing a Condition or Prescriptive Design Principle" in M. Egeberg and P. Laegreid (Eds.), *Organizing Political Institutions: Essays for Johan P. Olsen*. Oslo: Scandinavian University Press, pp. 59–78.
Howlett, M. and M. Ramesh (2003) *Studying Public Policy: Policy Cycles and Policy Subsystems*. Oxford: Oxford University Press.
Jones, B. D. (1994) *Re-Conceiving Decision-Making in Democratic Politics: Attention, Choice and Public Policy*. Chicago, IL: University of Chicago Press.

Lester, James P. and Joseph Stewart (2000) *Public Policy: An Evolutionary Approach*. Belmont, CA: Wadsworth.

Lindblom, C. E. (1959) "The Science of Muddling Through" *Public Administration Review* 19(2): 79–88.

—— (1977) *The Policy-Making Process*. New Haven, CT: Yale University Press.

MacRae Jr., D. and J. A. Wilde (1985) *Policy Analysis for Public Decisions*. Lanham, MD: University Press of America.

MacRae, D. and D. Whittington (1997) *Expert Advice for Policy Choice: Analysis and Discourse*. Washington, DC: Georgetown University Press.

March, J. G. (1994) *A Primer on Decision-Making: How Decisions Happen*. New York: Free Press.

March, J. G., J. P. Olsen, and R. Weissinger-Baylon (1986) "Garbage Can Models of Decision Making in Organizations" in J. G. March and Roger Weissinger-Baylon (Eds.), *Ambiguity and Command: Organizational Perspectives on Military Decision Making*. New York: Pitman Publishing, pp. 11–35.

Patton, C. and D. Sawicki (1993) *Basic Methods of Policy Analysis and Planning*. Upper Saddle River, NJ: Prentice Hall.

Putt, A. and J. Springer (1989) *Policy Research: Concepts, Methods, and Applications*. Upper Saddle River, NJ: Prentice Hall.

Quade, E.S. (1989) *Analysis for Public Decisions*. New York: Elsevier Science.

Simon, H. A. (1957) *Administrative Behavior: A Study of Decision-Making Processes in Administrative Organization*. New York: Macmillan.

—— (1991) "Bounded Rationality and Organizational Learning" *Organization Science* 2(1): 125–34.

Tversky, A. and D. Kahneman (1986) "Rational Choice and the Framing of Decisions" *Journal of Business* 59(4): Part 2: S251–S279.

Weimer, D. and A. Vining (1992) *Policy Analysis: Concepts and Practice*. Upper Saddle River, NJ: Prentice Hall.

Whiteman, D. (1985) "The Fate of Policy Analysis in Congressional Decision Making: Three Types of Use in Committees" *Western Political Quarterly* 38(2): 294–311.

Zelditch, M., W. Harris, G. M. Thomas, and H. A. Walker (1983) "Decisions, Nondecisions and Metadecisions" *Research in Social Movements, Conflict and Change* 5: 1–32.

5 Policy implementation

Implementation occurs at the stage in the policy process in which public policy decisions are translated into action. It has long been considered one of the most difficult, and critical, stages in the policy process for public managers—the phase in which any deficiency in the design of the policy or any vulnerabilities with respect to the external environment will become visible. Experienced public managers know that they will be ultimately judged on their ability to master the "art of getting things done" rather than by their good intentions.

This chapter offers an overview of the implementation challenges public managers face. It first reviews typical implementation problems that may be encountered in the policy process. It then draws selectively from the extensive literature on implementation to extract lessons learned for making implementation processes more adaptive and effective. In both diagnosing challenges and crafting strategies to overcome them, the chapter underlines two cross-cutting points. One is the need to build a concern for implementation into all phases of the policy process in order to avoid some of the most common pitfalls of policy fragmentation. The second is the importance of systematically considering the administrative and political contexts in which policy-makers are working in designing strategies to overcome the obstacles to effective implementation.

The basics of policy implementation

What is policy implementation?

Policy implementation is a dynamic, not linear, process. Changing policy rarely involves a straightforward mobilization of the resources necessary to achieve well defined policy aims that already have broad support. Instead, the implementation task can and often does involve elements of all the preceding 'stages' of policy-making and all of the uncertainties and contingencies that these might entail. For example, it may involve interpretation and negotiation of policy aims, as in the policy formulation stage, and may find implementers making decisions among significantly different alternatives that may affect the type of policy outcomes actually produced.

Implementation is also political. The implementation process itself not only creates winners and losers; but is also the stage in the policy process where the stakes of winning or losing begin to manifest themselves very clearly to many participants whose interests and desires may have been left out of earlier stages of the process. Agencies, and even divisions within agencies, may continue to compete for resources and control over implementation activities; and tensions may arise between the public, private, and non-profit organizations as they vie for influence and funds to implement government programs.

Policy implementation is also best seen as a form of network governance, since the defining characteristic of implementation is that it demands extensive coordination among an unusually wide range of actors. This is particularly relevant where integration of multiple policy objectives is sought through a particular program.

Actors in policy implementation

Implementation affects, and is affected by, a multitude of actors who define problems and solutions in a given policy domain, including many who may have been only marginal players in previous policy formulation and decision-making activities but who now may come to the fore.

Bureaucracy, with all its endemic intra- and inter-organizational conflicts, is a significant actor in, and determinant of, policy implementation. While politicians are significant actors in the implementation process, most of the day-to-day activities of routine administration are typically within the purview of salaried public servants. This is because, in the modern era, legal processes underlie implementation in all but the most flagrant instances of dictatorship or personal rule. In most countries there is a set of traditional, or *civil or common laws* that form a "default" or basic set of principles governing how individuals will interact with each other and with the state in their day-to-day lives. These laws are often codified in writing—as is the case in many continental European countries and other countries whose legal and political systems are modelled after European ones—but they may also be found in less systematic form in the overall record of precedents set by judicial bodies, as is the case in Britain and its former colonies. Even in common law countries, however, *statutory laws* are passed by parliaments to replace or supplement the civil or common law.

These statutes take the form of Bills or Acts, which, among other things, usually designate a specific administrative agency as empowered to make whatever "regulations" are required to ensure the successful implementation of the principles and aims of the Bill or Act. Acts usually also create a series of rules to be followed in the implementation process, as well as a range of permissible offenses and penalties for non-compliance with the law. The actual practice of administering policy in this situation is performed overwhelmingly by civil servants operating in various kinds of administrative agencies, such as ministries, departments, branches, and others, and by members of appointed boards and tribunals created specifically for regulatory purposes. They draft regulations to give effect to the general principles in specific circumstances, often in conjunction with target groups. Regulations cover such items as the standards of behavior or performance that must be met by target groups and the criteria to be used to administer policy. These serve as the basis for licensing or approval processes and, although unlegislated, provide the *de facto* source of direction and background to the implementation process in modern states.

The usual form of government agency involved in implementation is the *ministry* or *department*. However, other organizational forms exist. *Tribunals*, for example, are powerful players in implementation in many jurisdictions and circumstances and perform many quasi-judicial functions, including appeals concerning licensing, certification of personnel or programs, and issue of permits. Appointed by government, they usually represent, or purport to represent, some diversity of interests and expertise. *Administrative hearings* are conducted by tribunals in a quasi-judicial fashion in order to aid them in their activities. Hearings are subject to various kinds of political, administrative, and judicial appeals. *Public hearings* may be statutorily defined as a component of the administrative process. In most cases, however, hearings are held at the discretion of a decision-making or implementing authority and are often "after the fact" public information sessions, rather than true consultative devices.

Different bureaucratic agencies at different levels of government (national, state or provincial, and local) are involved in implementing policy, each with their own interests, ambitions, and traditions. Implementation by public agencies is often an expensive, multi-year effort, and continued funding for programmes and projects is usually not guaranteed but rather requires continual negotiations and discussions between the political and administrative arms of the state. This creates opportunities for politicians, agencies, and other members of policy networks to use the implementation process as another opportunity for continuing struggles from earlier stages of the policy process, such as policy formulation or, more often, decision-making, when their preferred solution to a problem was not selected.

But, while authoritative decision-makers, both political and administrative in nature, remain a very significant force in the implementation stage of the policy process, they are joined at this stage by additional members of relevant policy communities. *Target groups*, that is groups whose behavior is intended or expected to be altered by government action, in particular, play a major direct and indirect role in the implementation process. The political and economic resources of target groups, especially, have a major effect on the implementation of policies. Powerful groups affected by a policy, for example, can condition the character of implementation by supporting or opposing it. It is therefore quite common for regulators to strike compromises with groups, or attempt to use the groups' own resources in some cases, to make the task of implementation simpler or less expensive. Although this is typically done informally, more formal efforts are common in countries such as Sweden, Uruguay, and Austria, which incorporate regulator–regulatee negotiations in the development of administrative standards and other aspects of the regulatory process. Changing levels of public support for a policy can also affect implementation. Many policies witness a decline in support after a policy decision has been made, giving greater opportunity to administrators to vary the original intent of a decision should they so desire.

Analytical tools for understanding policy implementation

The set of tasks practically associated with implementation is best understood as a "continuum of strategic and operational task functions" (Brinkerhoff and Crosby 2002: 25). Tasks related to implementation must be integrated throughout the policy process, beginning with high-level "strategic" design considerations (such as constituency building) to more operational-level design and capacity building tasks (such as project management) in later stages of the implementation process.

Failing this integration, large gaps are likely to loom between policy intentions and actual execution.

Two of the academic founders of the study of implementation, Jeffrey Pressman and Aaron Wildavsky, captured the mood of early implementation research in the subtitle to their classic text *Implementation* (Pressman and Wildavsky 1973): "How great expectations in Washington are dashed in Oakland; Or, Why it's amazing that federal programs work at all." While we wish to avoid giving the impression that effective implementation is impossible, it is undoubtedly important to squarely face its difficulties.

There are two basic vantage points from which to view the gap between policy intentions and outcomes. The first perspective sees implementation from the viewpoint of policy-makers attempting to control outcomes at the grassroots. This so-called "top-down" view can be described as a "correspondence" theory of implementation in that it assumes a clear articulation of the intended policy exists and the conceptual and practical difficulty lies in how to transmit this intention faithfully down the line of bureaucratic command. Deviations at the field level from the intentions of policy makers count as an implementation "gap" or "deficit." Theorists adopting this perspective look for deficiencies in the way policies are communicated, and standards of implementation enforced, from policy-makers to field-level implementers.

"Bottom-up" analysts, in contrast, begin with the assumption that "street-level" bureaucrats often face an impossible task. Policy ambiguity, limited resources, and time pressures may make it impossible to implement policies as intended. To the extent that outcomes are deemed less than satisfactory from a policy maker's point of view, this perspective would look for the reasons in resource gaps, in the incentives embedded in the institutional environment faced by street-level bureaucrats, and in the understanding of their work and roles that such managers develop in response to often untenable implementation requirements.

Context matters greatly when assessing these potential obstacles to effective implementation, and when drawing appropriate implications for action. While a plethora of contextual factors may be important to a given case, four warrant special attention.

The first is the degree of political and policy stability. The environment for policy implementation may be considered "enabling" if there is relatively strong political support for the program outputs that are to be produced, and if bureaucratic capacity for analytical and implementation tasks is relatively strong. The second is the degree to which the external political and economic environment in which policy-makers are working is changing slowly or more rapidly.

How these first two factors—a facilitative general policy environment and the pace of change—intersect can offer clues for implementation prospects, which Figure 5.1 attempts to summarize. Where the environment is not particularly facilitative, and where change is rapid and unfavorable, public managers are likely to be restricted to "damage control"—keeping open the possibility of a more integrated and effective approach to implementation when the environment for it becomes more tenable. With greater stability in the environment, public managers may be relegating to "coping" or, at best, "scheming"; that is, identifying interventions to target for implementation that can serve as stepping stones of a longer-term, more ambitious approach should circumstances change. Where political currents are unsupportive of policy change initiatives even after official adoption, proponents of integrated

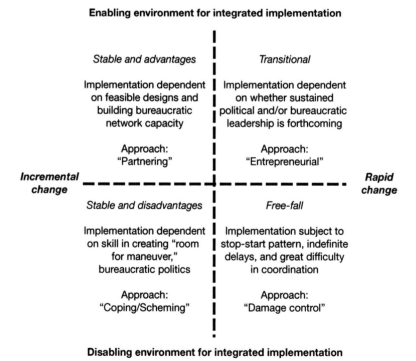

Figure 5.1 A typology of institutional change environments

policy-making are probably going to have to "fly under the radar," keeping the initial content as low-key and technical (that is, non-overtly political) to the extent possible, as they look for allies and wait for conditions to change. Where to look for such opportunities—how ambitious one can be during adverse times and in adverse environments—is a difficult question to answer in the abstract; but careful delineation of different stakeholders and their interests, as suggested below, may offer useful clues.

In more favorable conditions, coordinators of policy implementation may have more opportunities to build network capacities that will facilitate integrated approaches, and to identify and build strong coalitions supporting integrated policy-making in a given thematic area. Where change is fast, their approach will, of necessity, need to be nimble, even "entrepreneurial," looking for entry points that can serve to focus political attention onto areas for rapid action. Where the political and policy environment is more stable, building bridges to a wide variety of potential partners and focussing on overall network capacity may be the most important implementation strategy (the "partnering" approach).

A third contextual factor concerns the *openness of the policy process*—the degree to which the process is being influenced by a range of actors rather than having a narrow decision-making base. For instance, in a highly pluralistic country with a strong NGO sector and free press, policy-making will inevitably be shaped by a broader range of actors than a country in which policy-making is restricted to a small elite.

This distinction has practical implications for implementation. In more democratic, open polities, conflicts at the stage of agenda setting, policy formulation, and decision-making are likely to be relatively more transparent and regularized. This *may* imply that proponents and opponents of policies will be better identified—and may have reached more sustainable compromises built into the policy itself—by the implementation stage. In countries in which political decision-making is less formally contested, the politics of implementation may instead become "hotter," as actors who were excluded from decision-making strive to deflect policies with which they do not agree, or to steer them in a more acceptable direction, diverting them from their original objectives.

Finally, the *degree of public sector decentralization* is another contextual element that will almost always be relevant to consider in policy implementation. Decentralization is one of the catch-words of the development debates of recent decades, with most countries implementing, or at least endorsing, the idea of passing enhanced resources and authorities down to lower levels of governments (territorial decentralization) or to nontraditional, reconstituted authorities (functional decentralization). The extent to which such trends are present will affect the way decisions regarding policy adoption are reached, resources mobilized, and administrative and non-bureaucratic actors coordinated for implementation (see Table 5.1). Regardless of the extent of decentralization in a country, central-level actors—in many settings the most likely coordinators—will need to fulfill highly important functions: steering decision-making, monitoring implementation, setting and enforcing minimum standards, and providing technical assistance and

Table 5.1 Center–local relations and how they impact on implementation

Nature of decentralization	Bases for decentralization and their implications for policy decentralization implementation	
	Territorial	**Functional**
Within formal political structures	Devolution (political decentralization, local government, democratic decentralization)	Interest group representation
	Need to work with local governments in agenda setting and decision-making.	*Potential to incorporate variety of interest groups into decision-making forums for intersectoral development*
Within public administrative or parastatal structures	Deconcentration (administrative decentralization, field administration)	Establishment of parastatals and quangos
	Raises coordination requirements and potential for conflicts across sectors and between levels of government	*Potential to establish separate administrative authorities with integrated policy-making or execution responsibilities in a particular policy domain*

Source: Adapted from Turner and Hulme (1997: 153).

capacity building where local capacities vary significantly (as they usually do). However, particularly in newly decentralizing systems, central actors are not always well primed or incentivized to play these essential roles.

Challenges in policy implementation

Implementation is often neglected in practice and implementation failures are an oft-cited cause of policy failure or lack of success. Policy-makers often fail to prepare the ground systematically for implementation, resulting occasionally in high-profile policy disasters and even more frequently in policies that perform far below expectation. One key reason for this neglect is the sheer complexity, both analytical and practical, that implementation poses. Another reason is implementation's political sensitivity. In policy formulation and even decision-making, critical differences between stakeholders may be papered over by using vague language or even postponing outright decisions on mission-critical but politically or bureaucratically "sensitive" aspects of policies. This has the advantage of keeping a policy process moving forward and "buying time" for more supportive coalitions to be built. But the consequences of such avoidance become unavoidable during the implementation stage, in which public managers will struggle to generate, allocate and control resources, and interpret policy intentions. The intended outputs and results of a policy will fail to materialize, while negative side-effects of policies will become more evident.

The high degree of interdependence among stakeholders involved in modern policy-making process increases the complexity and vulnerability of the implementation challenge for public managers. As a result, the stakes in "getting implementation right"—in designing interventions that make successful implementation more likely, and in anticipating and building in mechanisms to overcome implementation difficulties—are particularly high for those who would desire to overcome fragmented policy processes. Such policy-makers must therefore build special attention to implementation problems into their calculations and activities from the outset of the policy-making process.

Drawing on a combination of the top-down and bottom-up perspectives, we can lay out some of the main conditions that may obstruct implementation processes. Table 5.2 uses the same three broad categories of analysis and action emphasized in other chapters of this book—the

Table 5.2 Typical implementation barriers

Problem	Description
Political (support and authorization) barriers	
Slow authorization	Plans and resource mobilization proceed very slowly due to the existence of multiple veto points among stakeholders in a network, making forward progress difficult.
Weak political support	Plans may proceed and even attain moderate levels of success in the pilot project stage while flying under the "radar" of key politicians with opposing interests, until program begins to "scale up."
Bureaucratic opposition	Key players in the inter-agency network tasked with implementing policy slow or sabotage implementation due to low priority of project, lacking incentives, and/or competing interests.
Poor implementer incentives	Local implementers (local government coordinating executives or front-line staff of agencies), who were not consulted during the decision-making stage, have inadequate "buy-in" or incentives to comply with directives from below.
Analytical competence barriers	
Vague or multiple missions	Intersectoral nature of plans and implementation leads to papering over conflicting goals or not clearly specifying tradeoffs in operational terms
Changing priorities	Tradeoffs made in policy decision-making—for example, between environmental and economic dimensions of a policy problem, may need to be reconsidered in light of changing economic and political conditions.
Poor design	Social or environmental programs that are unlikely to work as intended given multiple constraints left unaddressed by program design; failure is "overdetermined"—that is, it will occur if any of the constraints are left unaddressed.
Uneven feasibility	Different components of the integrated plans may be operationally linked—one can only advance if all are jointly present—subjecting operations to the "weakest link."
Operational capacity barriers	
Fund limitations	Funds necessary to implement approved plans slow to materialize, blocking progress, while in the meantime key elements of situation change "facts on the ground" and/or initial supporters of the effort lose heart and abandon effort.
Weak management structure or network coordination capacity	Poor precedents for coordination between major agencies— exacerbated in case of inter-sectoral partnerships—makes routine decisions slow and implementation dysfunctional.
Lack of clarity in operational plans	Approved and funded plans are mismanaged due to poor specification of roles, responsibilities and accountability. Problem is often made worse by poor oversight and information systems.

need to develop a coherent set of objectives for integrated policy-making, strong support and authorization for their implementation, and sufficient operational capacity to get the job done.

The first broad category of conditions obstructing implementation is *mission related.* The poor design of interventions implies that policies may fail even if implemented as intended. Or goals adopted in a multi-sectoral process may be too vague to meaningfully translate into operational programs and interventions.

A second category of difficulties involves the lack of adequate bureaucratic and political *support* for implementation. Support for policies can often stop at the rhetorical level, or at the agencies or levels of government that initiated them. Lower levels of government, and grassroots actors on whom actual implementation success hinge, may discover that they have little understanding of, or stake in, the policies they are asked to execute. Initial implementation may also trigger resistance to an integrated plan that might not have been predicted at the beginning of the process, particularly if not all relevant stakeholders had been consulted. "Political will" may begin to evaporate when difficult tradeoffs need to be made in practice, not just on paper, and as constituencies negatively affected by policy tradeoffs raise their voices (or even flex their muscles).

Finally, a range of *capacity*-related difficulties may have negative repercussions on implementation. Operational capacity is the bedrock of implementation. Many—perhaps most—ambitious attempts at integrated planning stop at the level of paper plans. The multiple types of capacity necessary to implement these plans often go ignored, or are optimistically subsumed under the heading of "capacity building requirements." Capacity includes human and financial resources, the institutional arrangements and procedures that underpin policies and ensure consistent delivery, and even the social capacities that help determine how social groupings will respond to implementation initiatives.

While all of these capacity requirements may be underestimated by public managers initially, implementation is particularly vulnerable to deficiencies in *network coordination capacity*—the ability of organizations to work together to achieve a common outcome. Coordination across agencies and—an even greater challenge—across sectors for implementation may be required in several different forms, such as sharing information, pooling resources, and (where activities fall outside the traditional gambit of any one organization) jointly implementing assigned tasks. Yet, coordination must overcome several common obstacles, well established in the literature, including the perceived threat agencies may feel to their autonomy from working together and the confusion or conflict over the nature of the task that stems from the inherently complicated, multi-sectoral nature of goal-setting.

Strategies for public managers in policy implementation

Policy managers interested in moving policy-making in a more integrated direction can manage their implementation activities in order to:

*   build constituencies supportive of policy change among a range of stakeholders, who bring different resources and interests to the table;
*   set overall objectives and design parameters for policies; and, at some point,
*   secure sufficient formal authorization and resources necessary to drive the process forward.

The implementation tasks facing leaders and managers under these headings involve the following:

*   *identifying* individuals and units within organizations that will carry forward specific plans and collaborations;
*   *operationalizing* broad policy objectives into specific, measurable targets that, in turn, are broken down into supporting tasks implemented by identifiable groups of people on a schedule;
*   *ensuring necessary operational capacity*, including attention not just to equipment and human resources but also to the incentives for grass-roots implementers to act as required for successful execution of the policy intention.

The key implication of viewing implementation as a process with important political dimensions is to underline that no single agency can be responsible for most implementation activities, and that the coordinators of implementation should be prepared to grapple with a serious degree of *confusion* (because of the large number of stakeholders) and *conflict* (among stakeholders who share some interests and compete in others) during the implementation process.

To make the leap from developing a coherent policy design to implementation demands *operational planning*. Operational planning is the process of developing initial and intermediate objectives and implementation targets for the interrelated interventions that make up complex policy change initiatives. Tasks need to be linked with specific agencies, and if possible individuals, as well as financial resources; implementation guidelines necessary for the effective interpretation of policies are also typically required.

Perhaps the most fundamental advice that can be offered to public managers regarding implementation can be summed up as follows: be aware of, and prepared for, the complex stakeholder dynamics you will face. Implementation of complex policy initiatives is *fundamentally* a challenge of coordination; and while coordination has a number of requirements, the prerequisite for dealing effectively with any of them is a thorough understanding of stakeholder interests, resources, and perceptions.

Stakeholder analysis serves as a basic analytical aid in this context. There are a wide variety of formats and variations on stakeholder analysis, but they share some common features: the delineation of all actors potentially concerned by, interested in, important to, or having any power over the projects being initiated. Such analyses also involve consideration of these actors' interests, level of organization, resources and capacities, and options for action.

Ultimately, policies and programs supporting an implementation plan must be integrated into normal budget cycles and operations. Before this can happen, coordinators of such efforts will have to be creative and entrepreneurial in identifying a range of sources of the resources necessary to get initial efforts off the ground. Resources necessary and sufficient for effective implementation rarely "report for duty" simply because agreement has been reached on some policy objectives. More often, they must be mobilized from a variety of sources, in a process that can determine to a large extent how effective and timely implementation proceeds. A recommended approach is to view resource mobilization as a constant and continuing implementation challenge rather than a one-off task.

An initial challenge in this context is the identification of "seed" or "bridge" financing and allocations of personnel that can enable integrated policy-making and implementation to get off the ground and initial activities to begin. To secure such initial financing often requires a hefty degree of negotiation with a range of actors, including government budget authorities and potential external partners. In the longer term, securing more stable sources of fiscal and other necessary resources often comes from initial demonstrations of success (enhancing the ease and attractiveness of such efforts to key stakeholders) coupled with a more official, legally grounded framework for the initiative and its continued implementation.

There are several dimensions to the capacity building challenge for network implementation. One is to decide on the appropriate structure to underpin implementation. Key options mirror those for the decision-making forums noted earlier, including allocating integrated implementation tasks to an ad hoc task force, an existing agency that takes on a slightly different set of tasks, or to a nongovernmental or private market unit via delegation or contracting.

Another network capacity building challenge is to develop—and use—effective accountability and management systems within the network. Accountability needs to be underpinned by an agreement on performance indicators as well as effective information systems that reliably update stakeholders and managers on the state of targeted outputs. Effective accountability must be linked to the mobilization of incentives and disincentives sufficient to motivate an acceptably high level of implementation effort. These are the classic instruments of hierarchical management but remain equally relevant in an age of network management.

Yet, accountability can only partly rely on such formal measures. The capacity of networks to implement policy-making in an integrated fashion will also rely on the density of relationships—the "social capital"—among local actors (such as NGOs, communities, local government coordinators, and line agencies).

Conclusion

There is never likely to be a "single best practice" associated with the implementation of complex policy initiatives, given the great diversity of country contexts, sectors and problems involved. But this chapter has underlined some of the ways in which coordinators of such reforms can improve their chances of implementation success. Policy managers will need to:

- Be prepared for the implementation challenge by using several analytical tools, such as stakeholder analysis and the consideration of the balance of center and local roles in implementation.
- Have a strategic roadmap for iteratively generating increased support and resources in the implementation process itself.
- Develop effective managerial and accountability systems that are facilitative of "network capacity," which is likely to be the

critical capacity necessary in multi-stakeholder implementation challenges.

Once a policy or program has been put into place, of course, public managers must be involved in its monitoring and evaluation, subjects addressed in Chapter 6.

Further reading

Bardach, E. (1977) *The Implementation Game: What Happens After a Bill Becomes a Law.* Cambridge, MA: MIT Press.

Barrett, S. M. (2004) "Implementation Studies: Time for a Revival? Personal Reflections on 20 Years of Implementation Studies" *Public Administration* 82(2): 249–62.

Brinkerhoff, D. W. and B. L. Crosby (2002). *Managing Policy Reform: Concepts and Tools for Decision-Makers in Developing and Transitional Countries.* Bloomfield, PA: Kumarian Press.

Grindle, Merilee S. and John W. Thomas (1991) *Public Choices and Policy Change: The Political Economy of Reform in Developing Countries.* Baltimore, MD: John Hopkins University Press.

Hill, M. and P. Hupe (2002) *Implementing Public Policy: Governance in Theory and Practice.* London: Sage Publications.

—— and —— (2003) "The Multi-Layer Problem in Implementation Research" *Public Management Review* 5(4): 471–90.

—— and —— (2006) "Analysing Policy Processes as Multiple Governance: Accountability in Social Policy" *Policy & Politics* 34(3): 557–73.

Hjern, B. and D. O. Porter (1993) "Implementation Structures: A New Unit of Administrative Analysis" in M. Hill (Ed.), *The Policy Process: A Reader.* London: Harvester Wheatsheaf, pp. 248–65.

Kotter, J. P. (2007) "Leading Change: Why Transformation Efforts Fail" *Harvard Business Review* 85(1): 96.

Lindquist, E. (2006) "Organizing for Policy Implementation: The Emergence and Role of Implementation Units in Policy Design and Oversight" *Journal of Comparative Policy Analysis: Research and Practice* 8(4): 311–24.

Lipsky, M. (1980) *Street-Level Bureaucracy: Dilemmas of the Individual in Public Services.* New York: Russell Sage Foundation.

O'Toole, L. J. (2000) "Research on Policy Implementation: Assessment and Prospects" *Journal of Public Administration Research and Theory* 10(2): 263–88.

Pressman, J. L. and A. B. Wildavsky (1973) *Implementation: How Great Expectations in Washington are Dashed in Oakland.* Berkeley, CA: University of California Press.

Robichau, Robbie Waters and Laurence E. Lynn (2009) "The Implementation of Public Policy: Still the Missing Links" *Policy Studies Journal* 37(1): 21–36.

Rondinelli, D. A. (1983) *Development Projects as Policy Experiments: An Adaptive Approach to Development Administration.* London: Methuen.

Thomas, J. W. and M. S. Grindle (1990) "After the Decision: Implementing Policy Reforms in Developing Countries" *World Development* 18(8): 1163–81.

Turner, M. and D. Hulme (1997) *Governance, Administration and Development: Making the State Work.* Basingstoke: Macmillan.

Werner, A. (2004) *A Guide to Implementation Research.* Washington, DC: Urban Institute Press.

Williams, M. S. (2004) "Policy Component Analysis: A Method for Identifying Problems in Policy Implementation" *Journal of Social Service Research* 30(4): 1–18.

Winter, S. (1990) "Integrating Implementation Research" in D. J. Palumbo and D. J. Calisto (Eds.), *Implementation and the Policy Process: Opening Up the Black Box.* New York: Greenwood Press, pp. 19–38.

6 Policy evaluation

On a daily basis, public managers are forced to live with the damaging consequences of various deficiencies in existing policies and processes, such as large gaps between political commitment and policy actions, poorly targeted and designed policies, and contradictory policy mandates. While the forces responsible for these deficiencies typically lie outside of the realm of influence for individual public managers, who may sometimes feel helpless in redressing them, these deficiencies can undermine their efforts, tarnish their image as hard-working public servants, and diminish the public support for their work. This need not be so, as policy evaluation can offer a critical line of defense against these deficiencies through systematic investigation of the effectiveness of policies, programs, and procedures.

However, serious efforts in policy evaluation, which can help to identify both deficiencies and remedial measures, are rarely attempted by public managers for primarily two reasons:

1. Evaluation may potentially harm a manager's reputation, resource base, or even career.
2. Evaluation is technically challenging, both in terms of the expertise required and also the data needed. As a consequence, many ineffective or even harmful policies continue to exist despite their less than optimal or even damaging consequences.

This chapter provides a basic overview of policy evaluation and is intended for public managers who are prepared to improve the effectiveness of policy outcomes through improved evaluation. Like the other chapters in this book, we focus both on the obstacles managers face in such an undertaking and also on the strategies available to them to overcome these barriers.

The basics of policy evaluation

What is policy evaluation?

Policy evaluation refers broadly to all the activities carried out by a range of state and societal actors to determine how a policy has fared in practice and to estimate how it is likely to perform in the future. Evaluation examines both the means employed and the objectives served by a policy in practice. The results and recommendations from these evaluation are then fed back into further rounds of policy-making and can lead to the refinement of policy design and implementation or, infrequently, to its complete reform or termination. Specifically, evaluation contributes to the policy-making process by:

* synthesizing what is known about a problem and its proposed policy or program remedy;
* demystifying conventional wisdom or popular myths related to either the problem or its solution(s);
* developing new information about program or policy effectiveness; and
* explaining to policy actors the implications of new information derived through evaluation.

Like the activities found in most other stages of the policy process, policy evaluation is as much a political as a technical activity. The purpose is not always to reveal the effects of a policy but sometimes it is employed rather to disguise or conceal a situation that might, for example, show the government in poor light. It is also possible for public managers to design the terms of evaluation in such a way as to lead to preferred conclusions regarding the merits and demerits of particular policy options. Similarly, actors outside government may make policy evaluations with the intention of criticizing government actions in order to gain partisan political advantage or to reinforce their own ideological preferences for specific kinds of policy interventions.

Actors in policy evaluation

As this suggests, policy evaluations are conducted by a variety of actors, both within and outside the government. Within governments, routine evaluation is usually conducted by the primary agency in charge of implementing the policy, described as "line departments" in many countries. The agency in question may have a specialized unit for conducting all evaluations. Most governments also have central agencies with exclusive or major evaluation responsibilities, such as the Government Accountability Office in the US. Comptroller or Auditor General offices in many countries also conduct evaluations, albeit usually only those concentrating on financial matters, but increasingly also of the more extensive "value for money" variety. Governments occasionally also establish ad hoc commissions to evaluate high-profile policies, and various judicial and administrative tribunals can conduct different levels and types of evaluation. Legislatures often have their own special units in charge of evaluation, such as the Congressional Budget Office in the US.

Given their location in lead and central agencies, public managers are often among the most influential players in policy evaluations. In conducting their evaluations, public managers enjoy several key advantages. First, they have access to information with regard to the implementation of policy, which provides them unmatched advantages in policy evaluation with regard to other actors, especially, for example, for providing information and opinions about the estimation of policy failure or success. Second, policy evaluation provides public managers with the opportunity and legitimacy to get involved in other steps of the policy-making process through their assessment and appraisal activities. Taken together, this allows public managers some leeway to reshape any subsequent policy redirection.

In addition to the numerous government actors involved in evaluation, however, there also exists an even a larger number of nongovernment actors. Researchers based in universities, think tanks, and consulting firms offer paid and unpaid (and sometimes solicited but also unsolicited) evaluations. The media also offer their own evaluation of policies, especially in instances when scandals or lapses in judgment on the part of administrators and policy-makers occur. The most important non-governmental evaluators are, of course, the service users who have firsthand experience of how the program in question is working on the ground. In addition, there is the general public, who double as voters during elections, and whose views on policy success and failure thus matter a great deal to politicians. Finally, there are the political parties, which offer evaluations of government policies in order to gain partisan political advantage.

Types of policy evaluation

There are many types of policy evaluation, depending on the nature of the policy actors involved in initiating or implementing it, the amount of information available for analysis, and what is intended to be done with the findings. At the broadest level, a distinction can be made between administrative and political evaluations. However, there are also judicial evaluations, although they do not usually directly involve public managers. Nonetheless, the impact of judicial decisions can have a large influence on subsequent administrative and political activities by prohibiting or allowing certain kinds of activities and not others.

There are five main types of *administrative evaluations*, which combine different types of monitoring and impact assessment activities on the part of public managers:

- *Effort evaluations* are attempts to measure the quantity of program inputs—personnel, office space, communication, transportation, and so on—all of which are calculated in terms of the monetary costs they involve. The purpose of the evaluation is to establish a baseline of data that can be used for further evaluations of efficiency or quality of service delivery.

- *Performance evaluations* examine program outputs—such as the number of hospital beds or places in schools, or numbers of patients seen or children taught—rather than inputs. The main aim of performance evaluation is simply to determine what the policy is producing, often regardless of the stated objectives. This type of evaluation produces benchmark or performance data that are used as inputs into the more comprehensive and intensive evaluations mentioned below.

- *Process evaluations* examine the organizational methods, including rules and operating procedures, used to deliver programs. The objective is usually to see if a process can be streamlined and made more efficient.

- *Efficiency evaluations* attempt to assess the costs of a program and judge if the same amount and quality of outputs could be achieved more efficiently, that is, at a lower cost. Input and output evaluations are the building blocks of this form of evaluation.

- *Adequacy of performance evaluations* (also known as *effectiveness evaluations*) compare the performance of a given program to its intended goals in order to determine whether the program is meeting its goals and/or whether the goals need to be adjusted in the light of the program's accomplishments. It is also the most difficult to undertake. The information needs are immense and the level of sophistication required to carry out the process is higher than is generally available in government.

Because of their greater specificity, formality, and focus, most administrative evaluations by governmental actors usually result in limited forms of learning, in which limited critiques typically lead to proposals to alter or reform only parts of existing policy implementation processes in order to better attain government goals (such as the creation of new agencies or regulations to deal with an issue raised), or to correct an oversight or error revealed in the evaluative process. These types of evaluations rarely result in new ways of thinking about a problem or new options for dealing with a program, and rarely propose to terminate a program or policy, because they typically take the existing definition of a problem and the government's preferred solution as given, and limit their evaluation to questions about the efficiency or legality of current efforts to grapple with a problem. While a recommendation to terminate a program or policy is always a possibility, it is a much less likely outcome of such evaluations than might be expected. This is due to the fact that programs and government expenditures tend to build their own "political economies," conferring benefits on some actors who can be counted on to support the efficacy of existing efforts and resist, or complicate greatly, proposals for straightforward policy termination. Such proposals, as a result, are typically moderated to propose modifications to existing activities rather than their complete cessation.

Political evaluations, in contrast to administrative evaluations, are typically carried out on an ad hoc basis by actors such as the media, think tanks, political parties, interest groups, community leaders, and public relations or lobbying campaigns launched by nongovernmental organizations. The motive for these evaluations is sometimes to offer independent advice but it is often to support or oppose the government, or to bring some issue of concern to the government's attention. In democratic polities, various interested members of policy communities and the public at large are constantly engaged in their own assessment of issues concerning them in order to better achieve what they consider to be the appropriate solution to a problem they perceive. Such informal evaluations—informal in the sense that they do not rely upon any systematic means for evaluation of carefully collected data related to policy impacts—easily translate into and affect formal evaluations in government since public opinion is an important determinant of perceptions of policy success and failure in democratic states. The need to face elections makes governments particularly sensitive to how the public assesses that government's performance in specific high-profile issues.

While some evaluative designs are more likely to produce more credible estimates of policy outcomes than others, in practice it is difficult or impossible to adopt the "best" evaluation design due to time and resource constraints. The evaluators should instead choose the best possible design by taking into consideration the importance of the policy, the practicality of evaluation designs, and the probability of producing useful and credible results. Wherever possible, public managers should try to bolster the evaluative resources available both within government and also in the nongovernmental sector.

In all cases, however, whether or not lessons (and what kinds of lessons) will in fact be learned by policy-makers depends on their capacity to absorb new information. The ability to evaluate and utilize new knowledge is largely a function of the level of prior-related knowledge that the evaluating organization enjoys. That is, having prior knowledge and experience with a policy confers on managers the ability to recognize the value of new information, assimilate it, and apply it to their policy ends. These abilities collectively constitute the "absorptive capacity" of evaluative agencies and agents, and should be nurtured and developed by public managers.

The scope of policy evaluation

Public managers can affect not only what happens to the results of evaluations, but also such factors as the scope of evaluation, including the nature of the actors involved in initiating and/or undertaking the evaluation, the amount of information available for analysis, and what is to be done with the findings. Possible outcomes of these processes range from maintenance of all aspects of an existing policy effort, to changes in policy substance and process to, rarely, policy termination. That is, the evaluations can involve simple assessments, through timely monitoring, of how established programs are doing vis-à-vis initial expectations, and of whether the assumptions underlining the policies or programs appear to be correct. Or they can aid in the launch of initiatives not only to decide whether or how policy initiatives should be modified, but also provide the information to defend the original proposals and records of achievement in subsequent policy deliberations. The scope of evaluations has several dimensions, as shown in Table 6.1.

Data and information for policy evaluation

There are two types of information collection methods that public managers should encourage in order to promote high-quality and useful evaluations: primary and secondary. Primary data are collected directly

Table 6.1 Scope of policy evaluation

System properties	
Integration of systems	The extent to which various facets of policy, such as economic, environmental, and social aspects, are considered in a functional and holistic way
Temporal systems boundaries	The extent to which the time horizon for policy-making is set
Spatial systems boundaries	The extent to which spatial boundaries are set to deal with interrelations between different levels and systems (local, national, and global)
Dynamic change	The extent to which dynamic changes and risks are taken into consideration
Capacity aspects	
Levels and limits	The persistence of a certain amount of quality of stocks of natural, social, and economic resources and capacities
Distribution	Distribution of opportunities, benefits, and burdens among individuals and social groups
Process aspects	
Cooperation and networking	The extent to which various actors directly or indirectly involved in policy-making can cooperate with each other, and to which knowledge and social networks are established
Participation and governance	The extent to which full participation and integrated governance are ensured in the policy-making process
Policy learning	The extent to which continual improvement and policy learning are facilitated and achieved

by the organization for the purpose of evaluation, while secondary data have been collected by outside organizations, typically for purposes other than the evaluation concerned. Examples of secondary data include national census data, financial market data, or demographic health survey data. Depending on the nature of the problem at hand, managers can demand more or less stringent or reliable sources of information, or focus on generating new information, or utilizing secondary sources. Each choice will have a significant impact on the policy evaluations that follow.

Evaluation can be based on existing data or require the creation of new data. Measures using existing data avoid additional costs associated with reporting and data collection, but may not measure as directly important individual and organizational behavior. Designing new measures based on new data, however, can be much more time consuming and introduce the possibility of collection and other errors that could, in turn, lengthen the time and expense required to generate significant results. Hence, it is best for managers to integrate evaluation criteria into program design right at the outset of policy design and consider these issues along with others related to the formulation and implementation of public policies.

Useful data can often be derived from budgetary or generally available statistical data, with little additional expense or time lost in independent data collection. Where this is not the case, it is often possible to externalize some of the costs of data collection—for example, by relying on other agencies to collect relevant data or to share costs and expenses with those agencies. Public service commissions, for example, may be prevailed upon to generate data on personnel issues that are essential for various kinds of technical output, effort, and efficiency evaluations.

Challenges in policy evaluation

The policy evaluation functions outlined above require either a highly trained workforce with future-oriented management and excellent information collection and data processing capacities, or the ability to outsource policy research to relatively available and inexpensive outside experts. They also require sufficient vertical and horizontal coordination between participating organizations to ensure that the research being undertaken is relevant and timely. However, these conditions are rarely satisfied, even in many developed countries, and serious efforts in policy evaluation are hampered by the following technical and organizational constraints:

1. *Lack of organizational support.* There is often no administrative mandate on evaluation, and there are often neither dedicated agencies nor sufficient resources to carry out the work even if official evaluation is required for major policy decisions.
2. *Lack of expertise in evaluation.* In many developing countries, as well as in richer ones, evaluation departments are often staffed by civil servants without prior training and experience in evaluation. Worse still, because of the low priority often given to evaluation, those assigned to evaluation tasks are often regarded as "incapable" of promotion to more operational-oriented departments, further undermining the legitimacy of evaluators and evaluation.
3. *Narrow perception of the scope of evaluation.* Much of the evaluation effort in many government agencies has been directed

to input-based evaluation in keeping track of various resources employed in policy implementation. Such evaluations are essentially bookkeeping in nature, and few evaluations focus on outputs, and even fewer focus on impacts.

4. *Lack of capacity in data collection.* Although this shortcoming is not restricted to policy evaluation, the strenuous data requirement of evaluation suggests that the impact lack of capacity has on evaluation work makes it the most deleterious. For example, the baseline data essential for any serious evaluation are often not collected before new policies are introduced, and there are almost no remedial measures that can be taken for this lack once policies are implemented.

The above technical and organizational constraints are closely intertwined with a set of political considerations, further diminishing the opportunities for conducting serious policy evaluation:

1. *Politically charged environment for policy evaluation.* The findings of policy evaluation, especially on key policy decisions, may have significant implications on elections and/or allocations of resources among different stakeholders and agencies involved. Some actors may also wish to disguise the results of policy initiatives and hence avoid blame for a failure or claim credit for a "success" (which might, on closer inspection, prove to be less successful than originally thought). A government may be so closely associated with a particular policy and have invested in it to such an extent that it might ignore contrary evidence of its effectiveness. As a result of all these factors, and more, developing adequate and acceptable methods for policy evaluation and "evaluating evaluation" itself are difficult and contentious tasks.

2. *Unclear goals and subjectivity in interpreting results.* Ensuring that learning occurs through evaluation is a difficult and complex task. Goals in public policy are often not stated clearly enough to find out if, and to what extent, they are achieved. In fact, policy goals generated through the political system are often deliberately vague in order to secure enough political support for their passage. The possibilities for objective analysis can also be limited because of insurmountable difficulties in developing objective standards by which to evaluate government success in dealing with subjective claims and socially constructed problems.

3. *The subjective nature of the interpretation of evaluation findings.* The phenomenon of policy failure is also neither so simple nor so

certain as many contemporary critics of policy and politics would suggest. Success and failure are highly subjective concepts and the same condition can be interpreted very differently by different evaluators, often with no definitive way of determining who is right. Which interpretation prevails is often ultimately determined by political conflicts and compromises among the various actors.

4. *Self-interest of public managers.* The desire on the part of public managers to use evaluation to enhance policy effectiveness may be constrained by their career aspirations and concerns for their agency's future. Unfavorable evaluation of the programs they direct may potentially lead to the closing down of their agencies and a restriction of their opportunities for promotion.

Evaluation strategies for public managers

Given these challenges, public managers can take several steps to help overcome them.

Clarifying evaluation criteria, benchmarking, and performance measures

Defining clear evaluation criteria enables evaluation activities to focus on the aspects of policy outcomes that are valued most by managers while eliminating excess bias. Policy outcomes are often multifaceted and different judgments can be made depending on which aspects of the policy outcomes are emphasized. Evaluation criteria provide standards by which policy outcomes can be evaluated.

Evaluation criteria are often defined with respect to the stated objectives of the policies themselves. For example, the success of a policy designed to reduce school dropout rates can be evaluated by gathering data on the changes in school dropout rates before and after the implementation of the policy. While focussing on stated objectives helps enforce accountability on government agencies responsible for policies, however, it may also lead to the dismissal of other related objectives. To ensure against such narrow evaluation, broader criteria would be appropriate. For example, a policy designed to reduce school dropout rates can also be evaluated on its impact on important economic and social development dimensions.

"Benchmarking" is a key method of determining the appropriate level of policy performance. Benchmarking is the process of comparing internal performance measures and results against those of others involved in similar activities. It is shorthand for a process of surveying other similar organizations and programs in order to assess "best practices" and the standards to use in comparing and assessing the performance of the agency or policy being evaluated. It involves a systematic effort to compare inside products, services, and practices to similar ones employed by outside leaders.

The crux of formal or technical program evaluation involves the design of quantitative measures of policy inputs and outputs allowing the determination of whether or not a policy intervention has made a difference (in the expected direction) in terms of the achievement of program goals. In its most rigorous form, performance measurement is the assignment of numerals to objects or events according to rules. This extends not simply to the measurement of outcomes as required by the many forms of evaluation cited above, but also to processes (as required increasingly by performance evaluation). The evaluation of efforts toward the attainment of policy learning requires the measurement of both aspects of policy-making.

The design of measures requires careful thinking and testing in order to ensure that measures actually link performance to organizational goals. Errors in the construction of measures can easily lead to inappropriate behavioral and policy alterations that might further inhibit the attainment of policy goals rather than promote them. Measures must be reasonably reliable, valid, robust, and cost effective. To guard against unintended consequences, multiple measures must be created that can be "triangulated" against each other to ensure that what is intended to be measured is actually what is being assessed.

The information needs of different policy evaluation techniques and the criteria used for monitoring policy progress and forming judgments about policy success and failure vary according to the specific type of analysis required. In most cases, however, policy evaluation requires the establishment or adoption of information systems and analytical units in order to allow benchmarking criteria to be developed and to continually assess changes in policy results on the ground. Enhancing the organizational capacity of the state agencies involved in evaluation is critical to assuring that learning, of any kind, results from evaluation.

Making greater use of impact assessment

Once measures have been designed and data collected, there is the all-important task of analyzing the information. This involves addressing directly the issue of what constitutes "good" performance; that is, how closely does a program have to achieve its original goals in order to be termed a success or a failure?

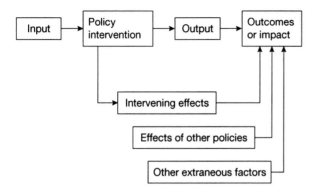

Figure 6.1 Central task of policy evaluation: distilling policy effects from other factors

Source: P. H. Rossi, M. W. Lipsey, and H. E. Freeman (2004) *Evaluation: A Systematic Approach*. Thousand Oaks, CA: Sage.

At any given time, the effects of a particular policy are closely intertwined with the effects of other policies and events, and thus the observed policy impacts are often the combination of the effects of a particular policy together with many other factors. Therefore, the central task of technical policy evaluation is frequently to isolate the effects of a particular policy from those caused by other factors, as depicted in Figure 6.1.

Too often, observed policy impacts are mistakenly interpreted as the effects of a particular policy under consideration, resulting in significant biases in policy evaluation. This is very often the case with political evaluations, for example, which typically do not carefully distinguish between policy causes and effects. However, this tendency is especially problematic today in many types of policy analysis, including more formal, technical ones, because of the greater need for identifying synergies and contradictions across policy measures involving many countries and aspects, such as those dealing with climate change.

Table 6.2 lists three commonly used evaluation designs used to isolate net outcomes from gross outcomes. Public managers often are able to exercise a great deal of discretion over these choices and can influence the depth and rigor of the review accordingly.

Establishing independent evaluation departments within government agencies

Public managers should understand the political nature of much evaluation but should also strive to enhance the quality (rigor) of administrative

Table 6.2 Evaluation design for isolating net outcomes from gross outcomes

Type	Description
Design 1: *Randomized* *controlled trials*	A randomized controlled trial establishes the net impact of a policy by exposing a group of people to the policy intervention in question (the experimental group) while withholding the policy for a comparison group (the control group). The allocation of people or units to the experimental and control group is undertaken on a randomized basis.
Design 2: *Simple before/after* *comparison*	This trial takes a single sample of the population and exposes it to a policy or program initiative, and the net effect size is measured in terms of the difference in the outcome of interest before and after the intervention is introduced.
Design 3: *Matched* *comparison*	In this design, an experimental group is exposed to a policy while a closely matched control group does not receive the policy in question.

evaluation, because technical sophistication will not only give them more leverage but also enhance the rationality of policy-making, focussing on the improvement of policies or programs that are in their best interests in the long term. They can, for example, set up monitoring and evaluation frameworks before policy implementation begins, building mechanisms to ensure independence in the evaluation (internal versus external evaluators) and better link monitoring efforts with impact assessment; and they can also conduct the evaluations and communicate the evaluation outcomes to main stakeholders.

One key way this can be done is by establishing or promoting the establishment of arm's-length or quasi-independent evaluation units or agencies. Such agencies can be established either within an existing agency or as an outside auditor. Internal evaluators have certain strengths, such as easier access to the data and a better understanding of policy/ program aims and experiences; but they may be biased. External agencies, on the other hand, enjoy the reverse situation: access to data is problematic, but independence of judgment is enhanced.

Improving access to program evaluation to organizations and researchers outside the government

Lack of "boundary-spanning" links between governmental and non-governmental organizations is also often a critical problem for successful evaluation. A healthy policy research community outside government can play a vital role in enriching public understanding of policy issues, and complements the policy analytical capacity found within government and, again, should be nurtured by public managers.

Consultation with affected stakeholders is as vital to policy evaluation as it is to other policy activities. There are many mechanisms for such consultations that public managers conducting evaluation might potentially embrace. These include setting up administrative forums for public hearings and establishing special consultative committees, task forces, and inquiries for evaluative purposes. These can range from small meetings of less than a dozen participants lasting several minutes to multimillion-dollar inquiries that hear thousands of individual briefs and can take years to complete. In many polities, political evaluation of government action is built into the system, in the form, for example, of congressional or parliamentary overview committees or mandated administrative review processes. While in some countries, such as the US, the UK, Australia, and New Zealand, these tend to occur on a regular basis, in others the process may be less routine, as political reviews are undertaken on a more ad hoc basis.

In designing evaluation processes, however, policy-makers must be aware of the appropriate locus for siting their activities in the context of the type of governmental regime in which they operate, and anticipate the kinds of results that can occur from both formal and informal policy evaluation. Policy evaluation processes should be designed to ensure policy "judges" are provided with enough information to be able to make reasonably intelligent, defensible, and replicable assessments of ongoing policy processes and outcomes. Public managers hence must ensure that accurate unbiased information is available to concerned individuals, groups, and organizations about their initiatives and impacts and, with this goal in mind, ensure that policy-making processes are thoroughly transparent and accountable, in order to discourage misconceptions about the role and intentions of government in implementing policies.

Participatory monitoring and evaluation (PME) is a process through which stakeholders at various levels: (i) engage in monitoring or evaluating a particular project, program, or policy; (ii) share control over the content, the process, and the results of the activity; and (iii) engage in identifying and taking corrective actions. It focusses on the active engagement (with capacity-building elements) of primary stakeholders to evaluate government efforts and outputs. Table 6.3 compares the conventional and participatory approaches to evaluation.

Table 6.3 Conventional and participatory modes of evaluation

	Conventional	Participatory
Who plans and manages the process?	Project management, outside experts	Local people, project staff, managers, other stakeholders
Role of primary stakeholders	Provide information only	Collect and analyze, share findings, take actions
How success is measured	Externally defined, mainly quantitative indicators	Internally defined indicators, more qualitative indicator
Approach	Predetermined, standardized	Adaptive

Focussing on potential improvements and learning in reporting evaluation

Unlike proposals for more limited reform, or simply the continuation of the status quo, the option of *policy termination* suggests a complete cessation of the policy cycle at a very near point in the future. Like more limited proposals for reform, consideration of this option involves the incorporation of the results of an evaluative process back into the policy process usually directly to the decision-making stage.

However, although it is fairly common for evaluations, especially politically motivated ones, to suggest the adoption of the termination option, policy-makers are typically very reluctant to take on this course of action. This is partially due to the inherent difficulties of arriving at agreement on policy success or failure described above. But it is also typical for existing programs and policies to have established beneficiaries and, often, to have become institutionalized to such an extent that their cessation is itself a costly process, involving considerable legal, bureaucratic, and political expense. In other words, although a problem may occasionally be seen as so pernicious that no possible option can reasonably be expected to resolve it—that is, that all reform options will fail—or as having been so successful that government action is no longer required, the attainment of unified opinion on these matters among relevant policy actors is very rare. Accounts of such events usually underscore the extent to which termination often requires an ideological shift in government and society allowing the uniform judgments of success or failure required for uncontested terminations to be made.

It should also be mentioned, of course, that a successful termination in the short term does not guarantee a similar long-term result. That is, if the perception of a problem persists, the termination decision itself will feed back into reconceptualization of problems and policy choices. If no other suitable alternative emerges, this can result in the reinstatement of a terminated program or policy, or the adoption and implementation of a close equivalent.

Regardless of the specific recommendations that emerge from evaluation, however, its main benefit is the learning that emerges from it. Good policy-making requires constant improvement and learning, and evaluation is the main place for such activity in the policy process. Learning in this sense is a deliberate attempt to adjust the goals or techniques of policy in the light of the consequences of past policy and new information so as to better attain the ultimate objects of governance. It involves a relatively enduring alteration in policy-making behavior that results from experience, and is what governments do in response to a new situation on the basis of their past experience.

There are four main types of learning, based on what is learned and where the lessons arise. Policy evaluations can contribute to any or all of these various types of learning. The four major types of policy learning are:

1. *Social learning*—the most general and significant type of learning, which public managers can promote and to which they must react. It involves fundamental shifts in public attitudes and perceptions of social problems and policy issues, and involves different types of actors, both inside and outside governments and existing policy subsystems.

2. *Policy-oriented learning*—a more restricted type of learning that involves the clarification of existing goals and policy beliefs based on experiences gained from evaluations of existing policies. It is the most common type of learning to emerge from typical policy evaluation activities.

3. *Lesson-drawing*—a more limited, means-oriented type of policy learning. It involves a variety of actors drawing lessons from their own experiences and the experiences of others in implementing existing policies.

4. *Government learning*—the most restricted type of learning. It involves reviews of policy and program behavior by existing actors and tends to be means-oriented at best. Its impact and consequences are generally limited to marginal improvements of the means by which policies are implemented and administered.

Conclusion

Evaluation is a key stage of the policy process and one toward which public managers should devote more care and attention than they commonly do. Managers are able to control or influence many aspects of evaluations, from the collection of specific types of data or information used in evaluations, to the design of benchmarks and performance measures, and to the use to which the results of evaluations are put.

Rather than shy away from participation in the evaluation process, public managers should engage fully in it. This involves not only activity at this stage of the policy process, but also the use of foresight to design evaluation right into the heart of the policy itself. With their longevity, experience, and ability to participate in policy-making from agenda setting right through to evaluation and beyond, public managers are in an ideal position to ensure that the policy process is one that features as much learning and improvement as possible.

Further reading

Bennett, C. J. and M. Howlett (1992) "The Lessons of Learning: Reconciling Theories of Policy Learning and Policy Change" *Policy Sciences* 25(3): 275–94.

Chelimsky, E. (1995) "New Dimensions in Evaluation" in *Evaluation and Development: Proceedings of the World Bank Conference on Evaluation and Development*, edited by World Bank, International Bank for Reconstruction and Development, Washington, DC: The World Bank, pp. 3–14.

Cohen, W. M. and D. A. Levinthal (1990) "Absorptive Capacity: A New Perspective on Learning and Innovation" *Administrative Science Quarterly* 35: 128–52.

Davidson, E. J. (2005) *Evaluation Methodology Basics*. Thousand Oaks, CA: Sage.

Langbein, L. and C. L. Felbinger (2006) *Public Program Evaluation: A Statistical Guide*. Armonk, NY: M.E. Sharpe.

May, P. J. (1992) "Policy Learning and Failure" *Journal of Public Policy* 12(4): 331–54.

McLaughlin, M. W. (1985) "Implementation Realities and Evaluation Design" in R. L. Shotland and M. M. Mark (Eds.), *Implementation Realities and Evaluation Design. Social Science and Social Policy*. Beverly Hills, CA: Sage, pp. 96–120. Later published in Rossi and Freeman (1993).

Mitchell, R. and S. Nicholas (2006) "Knowledge Creation Through Boundary-Spanning" *Knowledge Management Research and Practice* 4: 310–18.

Mohan, R., D. J. Bernstein, and M. D. Whitsett (Eds.) (2002) *Responding to Sponsors and Stakeholders in Complex Evaluation Environments*, Vol. 95. San Francisco, CA: Jossey-Bass.

Palumbo, D. J. (1987) *The Politics of Program Evaluation*. Beverly Hills, CA: Sage.

Rossi, P. H., M. W. Lipsey, and H. E. Freeman (2004) *Evaluation: A Systematic Approach*. Thousand Oaks, CA: Sage.

Sanderson, I. (2002) "Evaluation, Policy Learning and Evidence-Based Policy Making" *Public Administration* 80(1): 1–22.

Stufflebeam, D. L. (2001) "Evaluation Models" *New Directions for Evaluation* 89: 7–98.

Swiss, J. E. (1991). *Public Management Systems: Monitoring and Managing Government Performance*. Upper Saddle River, NJ: Prentice Hall.

Triantafillou, P. (2007) "Benchmarking in the Public Sector: A Critical Conceptual Framework" *Public Administration* 85(3): 829–46.

Weber, Edward P. and Anne M. Khademian (2008) "Wicked Problems, Knowledge Challenges and Collaborative Capacity Builders in Network Settings" *Public Administration Review* 68(2): 334–49.

7 Toward integrated policy-making

With an increasing population, recurring financial crises, widespread poverty, and deepening environmental issues such as climate change—one of the foremost problems of our time—the need for sound public policies has never been greater. These and other pressing collective problems are too vast for communities, much less individuals, to resolve on their own: only governments have the potential to address them. Yet the potential for effective government action is very often not realized, at least in part because very few public sector organizations are equipped to address complex public problems in an integrated, coherent, and adaptive fashion. To succeed, as the chapters in this book have argued, governments would need to change the way they define their goals, conceptualize and select alternative means of reaching the goals, implement their choices, and evaluate their performance. In this final chapter of the book, we reiterate these challenges and reflect on how public managers can mobilize to meet them.

To rise to the challenge of governing modern societies, above all governments and public managers need to recognize the complex and unexpected interconnections which exist and emerge among public problems. To deal with them adequately, they need to put in place institutions and practices conducive to responding to and accommodating the complexities of the problems they face.

In the following pages we discuss how individual public managers should approach their expanded policy roles in a broader context. These approaches not only characterize how the public managers interact with other players in the policy process, such as political executives, legislators, and fellow public managers, but also determine the ultimate success of their involvements. Such understanding is of paramount importance, as policy effectiveness achieved through the expanded policy role of an individual public manager may inadvertently undermine the work of others, and may even lead to detrimental consequences in a broader context. Such an understanding should also help public managers to be better prepared for the various challenges in their task environment that are beyond their control.

Such an understanding can also potentially increase the rate of success of individual public managers as they work toward the necessary level of coherence between policy goals and policy means that are required to better integrate policy processes and outcomes, and avoid policy fragmentation and poor policy outcomes.

Integrated policies

In public policy-making, integration encompasses two components: goals and processes. It is to be expected that societies will have goals that are competing and overlapping; these cannot be wished away. What societies can do, however, is to conceptualize them coherently so that they can be pursued in concert. There might be a need for trade-offs among the goals, but there may also be synergies that can be tapped among seemingly competing goals. But coherent goals in themselves are not enough—also required are integrated processes in order to match scales with efficient and effective instruments to achieve them.

To succeed in addressing collective problems, public sector managers need to have some conception of the collective goals they are seeking. A useful starting point is the three key concerns that all modern societies must take into account: economic prosperity, social equity and justice, and environmental sustainability. Although there may be debates on their relative significance, it is hard to deny that all three conditions are vital for social well-being. If economic policies, for instance, fail to take the environment into account, there will be consequences feeding back into socioeconomic systems. Similarly, if social or environmental protection policies do not take the economic ramifications of public measures into account, the resulting loss of economic welfare and the ensuing reduction in availability of resources will eventually undermine policy intentions.

Policy integration is not to be confused with policy effectiveness, however, because policies may be effective without being integrated. For instance, if economic growth is the overwhelming objective of policy-making and it is achieved, but at the expense of social stability and environmental integrity, then the government policies can be described as being effective rather than integrated. Achieving integrated polices is a more difficult task than achieving effective ones because of the need for maintaining balance across sectors.

Emphasizing the three broadcast goals of protecting the economy, society, and the environment does not preclude other goals from being considered vital. It is possible, indeed likely, that some societies would view national security or ethnic harmony, for example, as equally important goals to the three we have listed here. In such instances, they would need to pursue all of these goals simultaneously, increasing the challenges and complexities of their tasks.

Integrating policies serves numerous desirable purposes. First, it ensures policies are at least minimally consistent—and ideally synergistic—with each of the society's key policy goals. Second, it allows opportunities for identifying innovative policies that draw on the synergies possible among the key goals. Third, it allows opportunities for identifying any necessary trade-offs among objectives and for proposing remedial measures. Finally, efforts toward integrating policies increase the transparency and accountability of different stakeholders' attitudes toward different goals.

The nature of the relationships existing among these different policy goals is not always fully appreciated. It is common for policy-makers to emphasize differences requiring trade-offs and to ignore the complementarities and synergies among them. Social protection policies in times of economic crisis, for example, help to maintain a vulnerable population's income and serve as an automatic macroeconomic stabilizer, thus contributing to social and economic objectives. Similarly, taxes on polluting industries may promote rather than impede economic growth if they are accompanied by measures to encourage the growth of innovative and/or cleaner industries. Public works programs focussing on environmental projects during an economic recession can be seen as serving all three goals at the same time.

In practice, unfortunately, many efforts to integrate basic policy goals are often severely restricted. As the chapters in this book have shown, integrated policy-making is usually confronted with the segmented system of sector-focussed, time-constrained, and often politically driven policy-making found in all countries. Agencies responsible for specific sectors—such as agriculture, mining, industry, health, or social welfare—typically operate in isolation from each other. The second challenge is that social and environmental consequences often take a long time to materialize, while policy-makers typically have short-term time horizons. It is therefore likely that longer-term environmental and social dimensions of policy problems and deliberations will be ignored, while economic gains, which can be secured in the short run, will be highlighted. The third challenge is that, while assessment tools for projecting economic consequences are well established and relevant information is routinely collected, the same cannot be said for environmental and social consequences. As a result, such consequences are often poorly understood, poorly documented, and, hence, relatively likely to be ignored.

Integrated processes

Collective problems need to be consistently and continuously addressed in an effective manner, and this requires solid underlying institutions and processes. At a minimum, governments need integrated machinery for making, implementing, and evaluating policy. An integrated policy process is in fact a prerequisite for pursuing policies that integrate a society's fundamental policy goals.

It helps address the traditional "policy formulation–implementation gap," allowing critical deficiencies in implementing integrated policies to be identified at the outset. And it can help address the divide between decision-making and evaluation. Policy evaluation is not routinely applied to most policy decisions, and, when it is conducted, it is often motivated by procedural requirements or political considerations and thus fails to contribute to continuous policy learning.

As the earlier chapters have shown, public managers' efforts to integrate policy goals and processes will, however, come to naught if they do not take the political, organizational, and analytical contexts of their work into account. Policy-makers cannot escape the contexts in which they find themselves, but there are measures, discussed below and in each chapter of this book, that they can take to make them more effective in addressing pressing social, economic, and environmental problems.

The context of integrating policy goals and processes

Goals and design processes are not set in a vacuum but rather within particular contexts that differ over time and across space. The contexts impose constraints but also offer opportunities. As each chapter in this book has shown, three components of the policy context are particularly critical in determining the prospect of integrated policy outcomes: political, organizational, and analytical capacities. These broad contextual factors—consisting of numerous intersecting strands—constrain what public managers can do and what they need to take into account if efforts to improve policy integration are to succeed.

Political capacity

The political support that a government enjoys in society is a critical determinant of a public manager's capacity to develop integrated policy goals and processes. Political support is vital because managers must be able to continually attract both legitimacy and resources from their authorizing institutions and constituencies. Integrated policies may represent drastic departures from the status quo and conflicts over the nature and impact of such changes can be expected. Proactive political management, with carefully crafted strategies and measures, is essential for generating the political support needed to implement such policies.

Some governments and systems simply have greater capacity than others. "Strong states" (with strength denoting capability rather than authoritarianism) are characterized by cohesive internal organization —usually unitary and parliamentary forms of government with non-proportional voting systems or corporatist forms of interest intervention and aggregation—which are firmly embedded in the society in which they exist. Political systems that create multiple institutional oppor-tunities for confrontation, veto, and winner-takes-all policy outcomes slow down policy-making and promote short-sighted policy horizons. But political systems in which there is little opposition, and no real check on the exercise of government authority, are worse, as there are few institutional barriers to self-serving actions on the part of public officials, such as corruption and narrow sectoral "silo" approaches to policy-making. Democratic participation and accountability, without their counterparts of "antistatism" and multiple veto points, would in theory be most conducive to integrated policy-making. In other words, this would represent a political context in which the government enjoys the trust and support of the population it governs. Trust and support are often difficult to secure and retain over the long term, in political systems where the population is not allowed to participate meaningfully in both the electoral and policy processes.

Organizational capacity

Organizational capacity to make and carry out policies is also a vital condition for achieving integrated policies. While administrative capacity has traditionally been most closely associated with the implementation stage of the policy process, as this book has shown, it is equally relevant to the other stages of the policy process.

The nature and composition of policy communities, for example, have a major impact on the politics surrounding particular policy processes. The larger and more heterogeneous the policy community in a sector, the less likely it is to be able to make and implement integrated policies, due to the difficulties involved in securing agreement on objectives that go beyond the lowest common denominator. Governments wanting to promote export-oriented industries, for example, would immediately run up against the problem of which industry to support, because of the wide variety of industries engaged in exports and represented in the industrial policy subsystem. And this is even before any discussion of what to do about industries that would be hurt by likely increases in imports, and the social and environmental impacts of the policy being proposed. The situation is very different with regard to the telecommunications or banking industries, in which even fiercely competing firms are able to come together to take common policy positions, thus facilitating decision-making and implementation.

The narrow, sectoral focus of the participants in many policy processes is thus a major organizational barrier to integrated policy-making. Agencies responsible for specific functions are typically measured by the outputs associated with their own sector rather than broader policy goals. Agencies are deemed successful if they achieve their sectoral objectives, even if in the process they undermine other goals. Thus, for example, the performance of an agricultural ministry may be deemed successful if food production is increased—even if it was achieved through the promotion of large-scale farming involving the clearing of vast tracts of forestland and the extensive use of pesticides that seeped into the groundwater and imposed great costs on other subsystems and on the public. They would, of course, be viewed in a different light if the goals of integrated policy were applied.

An additional strong barrier to integrated polices lies in the poor quality of many public service organizations. For a wide variety of reasons, a large number of governments around the world simply do not have a public service that can effectively make, implement, or evaluate public policies in a coherent and integrated fashion. Lack of merit-based recruitment, promotion, and remuneration are often key reasons for a lack of bureaucratic capability. Political interference in ways that undermine morale and tolerance of widespread corruption are other reasons that vitiate capability. In systems with very low bureaucratic capacity, the likelihood of the adoption and implementation of integrated policies in any meaningful sense is indeed remote.

Analytical capacity

Analytical capacity, which includes the capacity to diagnose and understand social problems, is similarly vital to the success of policy efforts. What governments do, indeed can do, and the likelihood of their success, depend critically on their analytical capacity. Integrated public policies in particular require a higher level of capacity for analysis and judgment, capacities that exist to varying degrees in different governments.

Modern information technology has greatly reduced the costs of collecting and disseminating information. However, this enhancement has not always been accompanied by an enhanced capability to use the information. As a result, policies often continue to be made without the understanding of problem causes and solution consequences necessary for successful policy-making. This shortcoming is especially damaging to integrated policy-making activities because of the greater demands for coordination across policy sectors and the activities these require. Lack of analytical ability creates a bias toward maintaining the status quo or for measures that do not require sophisticated analysis. This is especially true for "wicked" problems, such as poverty and school underperformance, that require consideration of a large set of conditions and have uncertain or multiple causes and/or solutions.

This problem is compounded by the fact that often there are simply not enough people in the public sector with the required skills in public policy and administration to perform the complex tasks required of contemporary public managers. While the recent global expansion in the number of Master's programs in public policy and public administration constitutes a significant improvement in training, it will be a long time before these graduates will form a significant enough proportion of policy advisers, analysts, and managers to make a difference to policy-makers' mores and techniques.

The problem of lack of expertise is aggravated in many jurisdictions by the lack of information required to make, implement, and evaluate policies. The lack of data and statistics is especially acute in social and environmental matters. Without sufficient data, even the best-trained analysts are unlikely to properly understand the nature and extent of a problem, much less how to address it or to evaluate efforts to correct it. In many sustainability-oriented assessments, for example, the choice of indicators tends to be ad hoc and mostly qualitative, reflecting a serious lack of data to support integrated analysis. While the problem of reliable and comprehensive data on social and environmental matters afflicts all countries, it is especially acute in developing countries where statistical agencies are typically underbudgeted and insufficiently staffed relative to the vast developmental challenges they face.

An appreciation of the importance of these three capacities and their interrelationships helps public managers to identify critical gaps in a broader context, and also to understand how they can use the positions they hold and the resources they command to make a critical contribution to solving society's most pressing problems.

Overcoming the barriers to integrated public policy

This book has laid out several strategies that can be pursued for addressing the challenges of integrated policy-making. The joint consideration of all key policy goals—economic, social, and environmental, at the very least—should be a mandatory requirement if policy-making is to overcome problems stemming from segmented, sectoral policy-making. Simultaneous consideration of all three goals enables a fuller understanding of the policy challenges faced by society and how to achieve them. And a longer-term time horizon needs to be adopted to allow fuller consideration of environmental and social consequences along with economic effects. Taking a long-term view casts both problems and their solutions in a very different light, and opens up new opportunities for envisioning policy trade-offs, since addressing the estimation of costs and benefits can be spread over a much longer period of time.

The obstacles to integrated public policy-making may be overcome, or at least mitigated, by applying an "integration filter" to every stage of the policy process, as depicted in Table 7.1.

Table 7.1 Key functions and tasks of an integrated policy process

Key policy functions	Main tasks
Agenda setting	Place significant policy problems onto the government's policy agenda or examine existing and potential agenda items within an integrated framework that takes major interrelated policy goals into account
Formulation	Develop policy options that address the targeted issues in a way that is consistent with basic policy goals
Decision-making	Adopt options that meet the criterion of integrated policy goals and are acceptable to the broadest possible range of stakeholders
Implementation	Translate adopted policies into action, taking integrated goals into account
Evaluation	Review the implementation of the adopted policies against set criteria that reflect integrated policy goals

Application of the integration criterion to every stage of the policy process broadens the opportunity for shaping policies and for connecting the various stages of the policy process within a particular sector. This also brings together policy processes across sectors, thereby making integration a shared objective among sectoral policy-makers and public managers.

Notwithstanding substantial barriers, improving integration throughout the policy-making process is a goal worth striving for. Where barriers to integrated policy-making are greatest, for instance in "weak state" settings, welfare gains flowing from even marginal improvements to policy-making effectiveness may often be the greatest. Efforts in this direction, even where partially successful, may also support learning over time, and this learning may in turn provide a foundation for future gains. Public managers should dedicate themselves to this task.

Index